The Secret Sayings of Ye Su

The Secret Sayings of Ye Su

A Silk Road Gospel

Jay G. Williams

iUniverse, Inc.
New York Lincoln Shanghai

The Secret Sayings of Ye Su
A Silk Road Gospel

iUniverse books may be ordered through booksellers or by contacting:

iUniverse
2021 Pine Lake Road, Suite 100
Lincoln, NE 68512
www.iuniverse.com
1-800-Authors (1-800-288-4677)

The picture on the cover is of the Da Qin pagoda, which is believed to be of Christian origin.

ISBN: 0-595-33684-1

Printed in the United States of America

To Mr. Wang and Mr. Chang

Acknowledgements

For permission to reprint from copyright materials in excess of fair use, acknowledgement is made to the following: Coleman Barks for poems from *The Essential Rumi*, Columbia University Press for poems from *Cold Mountain* (New York, 1970), *Po Chu-I: Selected Poems* (New York: 2000), and *Ryokan: Zen Monk-Poet of Japan* (New York, 1977); State University of New York Press for *Songs of Kabir from the Adi Granth* (Albany, N.Y., 1991); Bantam Books for *The Bhagavad-Gita* (New York, 1986); New Directions for "9/9. Out Drinking on Dragon Mountain" and "Facing Wine" in Li Po, *The Selected Poems of Li Po*, trans. David Hinton (New York, 1996); Doubleday and Co. for Soren Kierkegaard, *Fear and Trembling; Sickness Unto Death* (New York, 1954); and Penguin Books Ltd. for *The Dhammapada*, trans. Juan Mascaro (New York, 1973).

Needless to say I must also thank Messrs Wang and Chang for giving the privilege of translating the text of *The Secret Teachings of Je Su* and my wife, Hermine for her careful editorial work.

Jay G. Williams
Hamilton College

Contents

Introduction

The Circumstances behind the Discovery of
The Secret Sayings of Ye Su

On July 31, 1996, I was attending a Buddhist-Christian Studies Conference at DePaul University in Chicago. I returned to my dormitory after an evening session, intending to spend a little time in the lounge watching the TV coverage of the summer Olympics. As I entered the lounge, I was approached by two Chinese men who, I would guess, were in their late sixties or early seventies. They were dressed in western-style, dark suits, but had very short-cropped hair that made me think they might be Buddhist monks. They were both quite short, I would say about 5'4" or 5'5" in height. They spoke simple, textbook English without great difficulty. I am sure they were Chinese because, later, they conversed with each other briefly in that language.

Although I wore a nametag that advertised my identity, they asked whether I were Jay Williams. I said I was. "The author of *Yeshua Buddha?*" Yes, I said, now somewhat surprised. They identified themselves as Mr. Wang and Mr. Chang. I assumed that they were conference participants, but I was to discover later that they were not registered for the conference nor were they members of the society. None of my acquaintances there had ever met them. "May we speak to you in private?" they asked. They looked quite harmless, so I suggested we go up to my room.

Once upstairs, they explained that they had "come into possession of" an ancient scroll written in Greek. Mr. Chang drew from his briefcase six photographs. The uncial text in majuscule[1] appeared written on a mildly tattered papyrus scroll that looked to be quite ancient. The words were separated but punctuation was at a minimum. There were no accents or breath marks. The upper and lower edges of each sheet were somewhat "erose" but the text itself showed little damage. There were a few little holes, but the letters lost (like an iota in a *kai*) were very easily surmised. My curiosity was obviously peaked.

They had apparently come to know of me through my book, *Yeshua Buddha*, and had concluded that I might have some sympathy for the text, though how they knew what was in the text they never explained. They also had apparently checked with someone who knows me because they seemed to think me quite trustworthy. Would I translate the text for them? I told them that although I had

---

[1] That is, with fairly large, rounded letters.

studied Greek and still use it occasionally, translation of an ancient document was not something I felt competent to do. They, however, urged me to consider the task and did not seem to want to take no for an answer.

I tried to find out where the scroll was found and if they knew where it originally came from. If they knew, they were not telling. Instead, they emphasized repeatedly how secret the whole venture must be kept. They had apparently taken the scroll to a Catholic priest (I gathered from what they said, in China) and he had copied the manuscript so that it could be easily read. He refused to translate it, however, telling them that it was highly unorthodox and unacceptable to Catholics. I spot checked his copy with the photographs of the scroll and found no obvious errors. Actually, the original scroll itself was fairly easy to decipher, so that copying it would not have been all that difficult. For reasons that I am still not sure I can articulate, I relented and said that it was conceivable that I might be interested in trying my hand at translation.

Much pleased, they then laid out the rules that the translator was expected to follow:

1.   The whole enterprise must be kept secret. I must not show the Greek text to anyone or ask for anyone else's help. When the translation is completed, the Greek text must be returned to them. I would not be allowed to create a copy of the Greek for my own use.

2.   I should work from the priest's copy. They would keep the photographs of the original.

3.   I would be allowed to copyright and share my translation informally with others. (In fact, they seemed to urge that I do the copyrighting, perhaps because they did not want their names made public.) I should not, however, tell anyone about the circumstances by which I received the document.

4.   Finally, they told me that if, after five years, they had not produced a published work involving my translation, I would be allowed to release my translation more formally to the public. I told them that without the original, the translation would not be worth much to scholars. They agreed, but said it had to be that way. My publication of the work, however, seemed a remote possibility, for it appeared that they intended to publish the text very quickly after the translation was accomplished. They told me that they would let me know when the work was in print and would send me a copy.

My guess at the time was that the scroll came from the west of China where there are desert areas and where ancient documents might be preserved. Since I know little or nothing about Greek epigraphy, I could not guess at the age of the work, though the Greek itself struck me as very similar to that of the New Testament. Quite frankly, had the Greek been of the later Byzantine Empire, I doubt that I could have translated it at all. Although I really do not know with any certainty either when the scroll was written or where it came from, my theory, which I will greatly expand upon, is that it is a "silk route" product and may be from the eighth or ninth century of the common era. My belief is that it is one of those attempts to bridge the gap between east and west for which the silk route has become famous.

I inferred from what they said that because all such finds belong to the People's Republic of China, the secrecy was important to protect the "finders" from accusations of stealing government property. There was every indication, since they confidently spoke of the work "appearing in the future," that they wanted to produce a version of their own for publication. It was agreed that if they were to publish my translation, I would receive credit for it. Nothing, however, could be put in writing.

After brief consideration and some mild protest about my lack of ability and the rather confining rules, I decided to accept the proposal as they outlined it. I packed the sheets carefully in my briefcase and traveled home, fully expecting that I would not be able to do the job and would end by sending the sheets of neatly written Greek back to their post office box in Chicago. I should also say that although they offered to pay a fee for my work, I decided to do it gratis, because my expertise is not in this area at all.

Much to my surprise (for my Greek was, in fact, very rusty), the task was not as difficult as I imagined and, after several months, I completed the translation. As per their instructions, I sent the translation, along with the copied Greek text, to a Chicago post office box. Thereafter, I received a telephone call thanking me for my work and expressing their pleasure in it. Since the reception of that telephone call, I have not heard from them. After a couple of years passed, I tried to write them at the same post office box to find out whether publication was underway, but my letter was returned, addressee unknown.

In any event, since more than five years have passed without any word from them, I have decided to make available to the world at least my part of the work. My profound hope still is that eventually the "owners" of the scroll will come forward and present the original text to the world so that it can be properly studied, dated, and interpreted. I am well aware that this translation in no way can replace a careful study of the original Greek document. Many will say that the translation by itself is historically quite useless. I would, to a great extent, agree, although it must be noted that many ancient documents from China are themselves translations from other languages and are not, in fact, "originals." Moreover, the teachings of the document have considerable merit in and of themselves.

Perhaps the very absence of the original will focus attention more properly on what *The Secret Sayings of Ye Su* really teaches. I myself believe that the work is of far more than historical interest, for contained in it is a rather startling reinterpretation of Jesus' teachings. Many of those to whom I have shown it would agree. Thus I present to the world this fascinating work, not so much as an historical curiosity, but as a living testimony to the faith. Whatever its source and provenance, it has, I believe, something to say to us today.

In most works of this sort, it is usual to begin with a long introduction and then the text, followed by notes and comments. I have decided, however, that it may be of value for a person to read the text first, then the explanatory material, and finally the notes and comments. The contents of this book, however, do not have to be read in the order presented. If you, the reader, would prefer, you may skip the text until you have read the explanatory material. Therefore I have arranged the subjects in the following way:

1. The translation of the text. The only alterations I have made in it since I copyrighted it several years ago is to change the name from Yeshua to its more accurate transliteration, Ye Su, to correct the spelling of Philip, and occasionally to tidy up the diction.
2. A description of the manuscript as I saw it in the photographs.
3. A preliminary analysis of the text's origin.
4. A discussion of the historical and religious background of the Religion of Light in the Tang dynasty.
5. A description of the so-called *Jesus Sutras* and the Religion of Light, the branch of Christianity which entered China in 635 C.E.
6. An analysis of the Buddhist and Daoist elements in *The Secret Sayings of Ye Su*
7. A discussion of the theology of *The Secret Sayings*
8. Notes and Comments about *The Secret Sayings*
9. A brief set of conclusions
10 An Epilogue.

Although this order seems reasonable to me, it may be that some readers may wish to proceed in a different manner, reading the explanatory material first before tackling the text. Others may wish to read the text with the notes and comments first. I will leave it to you, the reader, to decide which order is most helpful for you.

Jay G. Williams
August 2004

The Secret Sayings of Ye Su
The Translation

The Secret Sayings of Ye Su

1. To the multitude I speak only in parables, for the world is drunk with its own importance, addicted to its own pride. Drunken understanding is worse than drunken ignorance.

2. To you I will explain everything, if you will but sober up.

3. Peter said, "How, Master, can I sober up? Show me the way. Ye Su said, "To be my disciple you must renounce everything. Cleanse your heart of the world and its cravings."

4. Peter said, "Teacher, if I renounce everything, how can I live?" Ye Su said, "What I ask is not a law, for no law can demand the impossible. Only the Spirit can achieve the impossible. The world tells us that complete renunciation is impossible, but consider the birds of the air. They have no regular employment or storage barns; yet they live more happily than we. Renunciation is a work of the Spirit that never ends; it is freedom from the craving of the world. It is a life of genuine simplicity. It is the disenchantment of the world. Renunciation is repentance. It is to turn and go in exactly the opposite direction."

5. Do not think that I come to teach you about the Eternal Source. The Source is beyond all understanding. To speak about the Source is to create an idol. I come to proclaim the kingdom. Nevertheless, to live in the kingdom is to be one with the Source.

6. James said, "May I help you to rule the kingdom?" Ye Su said, "If you wish to rule, you are far from the kingdom and from me."

7. The kingdom is like seeds sown upon the earth; if the soil is good, the seeds will sprout and grow.

8. The seed of the kingdom is within you. Nourish it.

9. Philip asked, "When will the kingdom come?" Ye Su said, "When the time is full, the seed sprouts up and grows you know not how, but you will know when the harvest is ready. Only be sure that you water with care."

10. Peter said, "Show us a sign that we may believe." Ye Su said, "The kingdom is its own sign. Do you not know that the deaf hear, the lame dance, and the blind receive their sight? Have you no eyes to see?"

11. Mary said, "I love you, Ye Su." Ye Su said, "That is a good start; the kingdom is born from love."

12. Recognize the kingdom where it is. It is in the eyes of every person you meet. If you see the kingdom in me, you will see it everywhere. If you know the kingdom in any face, you will know me.

13. One day, as Ye Su taught his disciples, Peter left to quiet children who were playing in the courtyard and disturbing his concentration. Ye Su asked, "Where are you going?" Peter replied, "To make the children be quiet." Ye Su said, "Do not do that; let us go outside." The children were playing a game, laughing and showing great delight. Ye Su said, "Behold, the kingdom is like this, full of joy and gladness; let us join them." And so Ye Su and his disciples played with the children all afternoon.

14. Peter said, "Let us fast and punish our bodies so that the kingdom will come." Ye Su said, "Your body is the gift of our Mother. Treat your body with holiness and respect. It is not your body that causes your addiction; it is your psyche. Clean the inside of the cup; that is what matters."

15. Your body is the temple of the Holy Spirit. What other temple do you need?

16. Close the windows, shut the doors, keep the foolishness and violence of the world away. When your mind is free of foolishness and empties into the great Sea, then you will be close.

17. The disciples said, "Teach us to pray." Ye Su replied, "Go into your inner room and close the door. Do not pray in public as the addicts do, for that is idolatry. Do not try to tell the Eternal Source what to do, for that is presumptuous. Just listen. Listen, I say, listen. Those who have ears, let them hear."

18. Peter asked, "How should we live? Teach us the Law." Ye Su said, "The Law only cleans the outside of the cup but leaves the inside full of foul debris. If you think I have come with a new Law, you are wrong. The Law

was given for hardness of heart. The wine of the kingdom dissolves the hardness."

19. The world's addiction to the ego creates hearts of stone.

20. The world needs laws, for craving creates conflict, but when the kingdom comes there is only the law of love. "Love your neighbor as yourself:" there is nothing more that is needed. To love your neighbor is to love the Eternal Source.

21. Everything I say is of the kingdom, not of the Law. Sing and dance for the good news.

22. There once was a pearl merchant who sought the world's most perfect pearl. He traveled the earth, enduring great perils and sufferings, but returned to his home tired, impoverished, and empty-handed. Then his wife discovered the pearl he sought for so long in the headband he had worn on the journey.

23. John said, "Teach us about the kingdom." Ye Su said, "Do not look for the kingdom as though it will appear in one place or another. The kingdom is here, now. Nevertheless, you must prepare for its wonderful appearance. It is like a flash of lightning that illumines all. So do not close your eyes, even for a moment. The kingdom is like the leading lady of the drama who waits in the wings for her cue. She is there, but you do not see her."

24. The world is addicted, always craving, never satisfied. Because the world craves, there is suffering and violence and hate. Those who succeed in the world are the unhappiest of all.

25. Do not despise the world or its people; the seeds of the kingdom are everywhere. Delight in everything.

26. Peter said, "Some effeminate men wanted to see you but I sent them away." Ye Su said, "You were wrong to do that, Peter. Did I not tell you that the seeds of the kingdom are everywhere?" "But suppose they will not reform their ways?" "Think not of the faults of others, Peter, for no one has achieved true righteousness. Have more faith in the power of the kingdom. Therefore I say, do not judge others or censure them. Look only to your own craving."

27. Nathaniel asked, "Must we become celibate for the sake of the kingdom?" Ye Su said, "No, sexual desire is a gift from our Mother and we must give thanks for her gifts and use them wisely. Celibacy does not end the craving but only intensifies it. True marriage is the reunification of Adam, and is the great and holy Mystery. Only the Child of Adam enters the kingdom."

28. I am the light that shines in the darkness, the light that enlightens every person. You have always known me, though today, in your blindness, you do not recognize me.

29. Only the naked should baptize the naked.

30. Running floodwaters of the earth and the unpredictable winds of heaven; a plunge of death into the waters, the fluttering of the dove: the Child of Adam is born.

31. Peter said, "Why do you allow women to follow you? Should not only men be disciples?" Ye Su said, "Peter, Peter, are you so blind? Do you not see that the seeds of the kingdom are planted in both women and men and that in the kingdom there is no difference between them? We are all the union of male and female and therefore are in ourselves both male and female. Until you realize that, the kingdom will be far away. To remind you of your blindness, when I appear in glory, Mary shall see me first. She is my beloved disciple."

32. The kingdom is *agape* made manifest among us. It is the one great miracle. If you know *agape*, the kingdom comes.

33. *Agape* is not just a feeling in the human heart but grows among us. Act in *agape*; then there will be feeling.

34. Judas asked, "What should we do for the poor?" Ye Su answered, "Love the poor, but do not pity them. They are much closer to the kingdom than are the rich. Do not think that the end of life is worldly goods. It is the things of the world that blind us to the kingdom. But feed the hungry and care for the suffering as you would care for your own mother or father or wife or friend. Watch for the kingdom, for it is there, among the poor. The glory is revealed among the homeless, for the Child of Adam has nowhere to lay his head."

35. Weep for the rich, for it is easier for a camel to pass through the eye of a needle than for a rich man to enter the kingdom.

36. The true gifts of the Magi I give you: compassion, simplicity, and dare not be first in the world.

37. The kingdom is like an ancient well which flows with living water. Draw up the water and quench your thirst.

38. Trust in the kingdom. That is all that is needed.

39. From the Source flows the One and the One contains the Two. The Two give birth to the Third, the Child of Adam, and from the Three flow forth all things.

40. All flows creatively from the Source. When you create, the power of the Source is yours. Music, Poetry, Art are gifts of the Source.

41. John said, "Teach us about the Spirit." Ye Su said, "The Spirit is the kingdom made manifest. When the trees move their branches you know that the Spirit is there. The Spirit is your life. When you breathe, it is the Spirit that moves within you. When your breath flows perfectly with the Spirit, you are in the kingdom. Watch your breath."

42. James said, "Our enemies surround us and want to destroy the kingdom. How shall we fight against our enemies? Shall we take up arms?" Ye Su said, "Love your enemies; do good to those who misuse you, for in them dwells also the kingdom. And forgive, always forgive." "But," said James, "suppose that they should kill us?" Ye Su replied, "No one can kill the kingdom for it has been from the beginning and will be until the end. As for the rest, it is mortal and will return to the Mother. Do not cling to life. Life and death are twin sisters who can never be separated. Death too is a blessing. But enter the kingdom where there is eternal life."

43. In all things be mindful.

44. "Is my soul immortal? Will I go to heaven?" asked John. "Your *psyche*," said Ye Su, "is a function of your body and like your body will

return to dust. But the kingdom of light is everlasting. Enter the kingdom of light and find eternal *shalom*."

45. I will die and on the third day will burst forth again from the tomb. The kingdom of light can be hidden for a time, but cannot be destroyed, not by the so-called religious authorities, not by the great world empires. If you trust in the kingdom, you will not fear death.

46. Peter said, "Teacher, I hope and pray you will not die." Ye Su said, "If you wish to enter the kingdom, you must die, for new life comes only from death. Peter, all component parts decay. Your *psyche* will crumble into dust, but if your trust is into the light, you will rest in the light. Like me, you will burst forth again from the tomb. The light is eternal."

47. Judas said, "Teacher, the prophets taught us that the Eternal demands justice for all. Should we not organize to fight against the injustice in our society?" Ye Su said, "*Agape* demands justice in the world and woe to the person who does not seek to right the wrongs of society. But *agape* also knows that justice without the kingdom is hollow and unstable. In this world of craving, injustice will always reign because craving demands injustice. To think that there can be true justice without the coming of the kingdom is an illusion."

48. The kingdom comes from the glory of the Eternal, Incomprehensible Source.

49. Judas said, "Let us organize ourselves with a president and officers so that our movement may be more effective." Ye Su said, "*Agape* does not hold to order. The more you organize, the more your organization will become but one more institution of craving. Soon you will have some men ruling over others. Some will be forced to bow to their masters. There will be ordinances and taboos. People will begin to think that faith is just subscribing to a set of ideas and the kingdom will become a fossil to be put upon the shelf along with all the other archaic doctrines. Then there will be persecutions and wars carried out in my name as the blind lead the blind into disaster. No, Judas, call no person Father or Rabbi or the Reverend or your Holiness. All of this comes from the craving of the world and will

only end in violence and disorder. The kingdom comes as a miracle and miracles cannot be contained."

50. When you meet, meet as friends. Love one another. Celebrate *agape*.

51. Proclaim the good news of the eternal kingdom but think not of proselytes. The kingdom will provide the miracle.

52. Do not think that a tribe or nation or empire can become the kingdom, for the kingdom will grow when and where it wills. Nothing will impede the kingdom more than a nation of addicts pretending to be the kingdom.

53. I looked and I saw a great beast rising out of the earth, devouring everyone in its path. Great was its pride and great its claims to truth. To those whom it enticed it offered holy feelings and future hopes, but it attacked the very kingdom it proclaimed. Those who were devoured seldom returned. The name of the beast was the Holy Church.

54. Keep my teachings secret; cast no pearls before swine, lest the great beast overhear the words and destroy.

55. To live in the kingdom is to laugh and be glad. There is no soberness in the realm of light; it is freedom, hope, and joy.

56. I do not come to judge the world or anyone in it. I come to reveal the light of the kingdom. Those who turn from the light and seek the darkness condemn themselves and enter the darkness. Those who seek the light are of the light. Trust in the light and the healing is yours.

57. Do not judge others. If they seek the darkness, that is their danger, their woe. But trust the light and it will grow into a great flame. Let your light shine before all people that they may see and trust also.

58. James said, "There are other teachers in other lands who offer wisdom to the world. How should we think of them?" Ye Su said, "The seeds of the kingdom are everywhere. Do not think of the kingdom as your personal possession. My light is to be found everywhere in the world and many are those who have found me. But beware the influence of humanity's dark

craving. Traditions of humanity are few that have not become corrupted by the craving. But where there is light, rejoice in it."

59. One night Ye Su gathered those he taught and led them to an inner room set apart. There, at dinner, he took a loaf of bread and broke it before them, "This bread," he said, "is a gift from the Mother of us all. Together we share her matter. This loaf also comes from the sunlight of the Father's heavenly realm, now broken that we may become one in the heavenly light. Together we share the bread of heaven and earth; the kingdom of love is among us; this is my body."

60. The kingdom does not belong to individuals. It becomes manifest in *agape* shared. Therefore the loaf must be broken so that *agape* may be known in the sharing.

61. Ye Su also took a cup of wine, rich in aroma and body, and said, "This wine is a gift from our Mother to make glad the hearts of humans, so that we may know joy and *shalom*. It is likewise a gift from the sun from the Father's heavenly realm. It reminds us of the great transformation which the light and love of the kingdom bring. This is my blood poured out. In the world, wine may bring drunkenness; here one finds the kingdom."

62. I am the True Light, glowing from the Eternal Source. Cleave the wood, I am there; lift the stone, I am there.

63. Ye Su asked Mary, "What shall you do when I return from the dead?" Mary said, "If you were to return from the dead, I would observe awe-struck silence and speak to no one about it." Ye Su said, "You have learned well, Mary. You shall be my apostle."

64. Have you not heard that it was said of old, "Those who speak do not know, those who know do not speak."

65. Peter said, "But we must say *something*. How can we proclaim the good news if we can say nothing?" Ye Su smiled but did not speak. Then he led his disciples in the Circular Dance of Joy that they danced until the dawn.

66. Ye Su hung upon the tree of life. He chanted the ancient psalms as blood dripped from his hands and feet. He spoke words of *shalom* to those who had not run away in fear. He encouraged and forgave. The earth trembled

and the heavens grew dark. The Mother sobbed and the Father mourned. But in the midst of the trembling there was serenity; in the midst of darkness there was tremendous light streaming from every pore of his body, radiating to every corner of the earth. In death, life is born; in darkness, there is a dawning.

67. Death came, the tomb was made ready and then, after the burial, sealed. But nothing can hold the light. At any moment it can burst forth with an unimaginable radiance. And it does.

68. And you must die. Your craving, born of your prideful ego, must perish. Your death, like that of Ye Su, will be dreadfully painful, for the addiction is so intense and has gone on so long. Earth will tremble and Heaven will grow dark before the veil is rent, the Holy of Holies revealed, and the light, the eternal light, begins to shine.

69. The Well, the Water, and the Drink of Eternity: the three are one.

70. I Am the Way, the Truth, and the Life. In every part of the world those who know, know me. I am the wise man's treasure and the lost man's refuge.

71. To you I leave the gifts of the Spirit: *agape*, simplicity, and *shalom*. The kingdom of light is here. It is time to rejoice.

72. Take care to whom these words are given, for those of the world will laugh and deride and then use them for their own worldly ends. Hide my secrets until the time is fulfilled. Beware the beast.

The Document

The Nature of the Document

I must begin by underlining the fact that I only had the opportunity to view the photographs of the scroll for a few minutes. I did not have access to the original nor did I have instruments to measure what I saw. Here, at least, is what I did note:

1. The text, I would guess, is written on papyrus, with the lines horizontal, that is, *in recto*. I was told that the photographs were approximately the same size as the original. I would guess that the height is about 36 centimeters and the width, about 32 centimeters. That is, the height is a little more than the width and both are slightly more than a foot.

2. The writing is rather rust colored, but quite legible. It is, as already has been said, uncial in majuscule.

3. Each page, except the last, contains two columns. Page six has only part of one column.

4. The writing is fairly small but in majuscule. There are no breath marks or accents but the words are slightly separated. I have looked at photographs of other ancient manuscripts and I would say the calligraphy is most reminiscent of the Chester Beatty papyri [See William Henry Paine Hatch, *The Principal Uncial Manuscripts of the New Testament* (Chicago: University of Chicago Press, 1939), Plate II.]

5. Only a few letters are obscured by holes and these are easily restored.

6. The language of the text is, on the whole, very similar to the synoptic gospels. The only strange feature is that the name Ye Su receives no appropriate endings. Therefore, the title of the work is simply *Oi Logoi Kruptoi Ye Su* (The Secret Words of Ye Su). It should be noted that Ye Su (耶穌) is the Chinese name for Jesus.[2] In my original translation, I rendered the name Yeshua, but I have decided now to retain the original, simpler Ye Su.

---

2 It is interesting that the characters pronounced Ye Su have the following meaning. Ye is simply a final interrogative particle, denoting a question, while Su means to revive or come to. Hence the name seems to question Ye Su's revival or resurrection.

7. There are seventy-two sayings which, in the original manuscript are separated slightly but unnumbered. I have supplied numbers for ease in reference. Whether the number seventy-two (12x6) has any special significance is a question that might be explored.

8. Whether this manuscript was part of a larger scroll I could not determine from the photographs. It may be noteworthy that although the right side of page one and the top and bottom of each page is somewhat erose, the right side of page six is not. This could indicate that it was or is attached to something else that was not copied.

9. The state of preservation, which is excellent, indicates that it was stored in a very dry place and that would suggests either a desert region or a hermetically sealed jar or both.

10. There was no date or name of author as is common among Chinese manuscripts

The Text's Provenance: Preliminary Considerations

The first question that might be asked about the text is: Is this text a modern forgery? Forgery, however, appears to be the wrong word, for a forgery claims to be something that it is not. It must be emphasized that Messrs. Wang and Chang made no claims at all. They indicated that they thought the document important, but would offer no clues as to its age or provenance. They were not trying to "pass this work off" as something from any particular time. They simply asked to have it translated. The text itself makes no claims either. Unlike many apocryphal gospels it does not purport to have been written by a disciple.

Moreover, it seems unlikely to me that anyone would have gone to such trouble to deceive me. Although I could be mistaken, the writing material looked very much like papyrus and the writing itself ancient. Why would anyone go to such pains to produce the text of which I saw photographs? And if they wanted to deceive the world, why come to me? The whole event was so strange and the document so unusual that I just cannot believe someone concocted it. My conclusion is that the document is, in some sense, genuine, whatever that may mean.

The fact that the work is not a forgery, however, does not solve the problem of where it came from or why it is written in Greek. Its language might seem to indicate that it is a document brought to China by Western missionaries, except for one obvious fact: the work, though it is about Ye Su (Jesus) and shows good acquaintance with the Bible, incorporates Daoist and Buddhist ideas and it seems very unlikely that these were developed independently in the West. Clearly this is a work of synthesis that presents Ye Su in Chinese form. Although written in a western language, the text seems directed toward a Chinese audience.

Quite frankly, I was quite stymied by all this. Nothing seemed to make much sense. Then I happened upon *The Jesus Sutras*, a work by Martin Palmer published in 2001 that provided for me a whole new vista for understanding the history of Christianity in East Asia.[3] Among the most fascinating subjects discussed in the book is the discovery, some fifty miles from Xian,[4] of a tower or pagoda dating from the eighth

---

3 Palmer, *The Jesus Sutras: Recovering the Lost Scrolls of Taoist Christianity*. Actually much of what he presents is not particularly new, for both the Great Stele and what he calls the Jesus Sutras have been known for a long time. Nevertheless, Palmer gives these documents a contemporary interpretation that reopens the whole matter for new investigation.

4 All Chinese names will be put in Pinyin rather than Wade-Giles.

century that, in origin, was Christian. This corroborates the information on the stele to be mentioned below that Christianity was already known in China by the Tang dynasty period, brought to the Middle Kingdom by missionaries from the Church of the East. In China the Christian movement was known as *Jing Jiao* (景教) a title translated by Martin Palmer as "The Religion of Light (or the Luminous Religion) from the West."

Because "the Religion of Light" seems to be the commonly accepted name, I shall use it throughout this book. Readers, however, should know, first of all, that *jiao*, which is translated as "religion," really would be better rendered "teaching." More important is the fact that the character used on the stele that is translated "light" is a strange one and is certainly not familiar to the modern Chinese reader.[5] One might expect either ming (明) or guang (光) Instead the stele uses a character that does not seem to have been common at all. In fact, many scholars believe that it is the miswriting of another character (*jing*) that means today, in the first instance, "scenery." It also, as an adjective, can mean "grand." Thus it was used in the fourth century B.C.E. of Mengzi (better known in the west as Mencius) as an honorific. So the tradition could have been called simply the "Grand" or perhaps "Revered" Teaching. There are some indications, however, that the word in the Tang dynasty had some connection to both sunlight and shadow.

If the usual emendation of the character is made, the radical for it is the sun and the phoneme that of a shadow. One possible interpretation is that the teaching is like the shadow that the sun casts. The teaching witnesses to the light, for, in a sense, it reveals its presence by its absence. Perhaps, however, this interpretation is too speculative. In any event, because of the emphasis upon light in the document I translated, this name alone was enough to catch my attention.

By way of introducing the Religion of Light, Palmer describes the Church of the East that brought the faith to the Middle Kingdom. Perhaps the most important feature of that church is that it never came under the jurisdiction of the Roman Empire. Although for many years nominally under the Patriarch of Antioch, in 424 C.E. the Church of the East, which centered in Mesopotamia and Persia, broke from the Western Church and founded its own patriarchy. Not long after that Nestorius, the Bishop of Constantinople (d. 451), was declared a heretic and many of his followers moved to the East, founding a major theological center in Nisibis. The teaching of Nestorius, which, quite frankly, did not differ that much

---

[5] For a now old but still serviceable discussion, see Saeki, *The Nestorian Monument in China*, 183 ff.

from the orthodox position worked out at the Council of Chalcedon, became influential in the Mesopotamia. Because the Church of the East did not conform to decisions made in the West, it was considered heretical by the Western Churches and was often branded with the name of the heretic, Nestorius. In fact, however, the Church existed long before Nestorius and was not a product of his "heresy." Within the Church of the East a variety of theological positions were held beside Nestorianism, so that it is really incorrect to call it by that name.[6]

The Western Church, in many ways a product of the Roman/Byzantine Empire, was uneasy about such a large church existing outside of its political and ecclesiastical control. The Church of the East, on the other hand, was happy to distance itself from the West because Byzantium was, for Persia, the enemy. To be too cooperative with Constantinople would have raised cries of sedition. Therefore, there were members of the Church of the East who were quite content to be called Nestorians (i.e. heretics) by the Western Church.

During its heyday, the Church of the East was quite successful in the regions east of the Roman Empire, flowering in Mesopotamia, Iran, and central Asian countries and extending its influence into both India and China. Before the advent of Islam, it was a growing and prospering community with its own Patriarch, ten metropolitan sees and ninety-six bishoprics. Persia (Iran) was close to being predominantly Christian before Islam arrived and even after that religion made converts, large communities of Christians remained.

It should be noted, however, that in 632 C.E., just three years before the Religion of Light entered China, the Sassanian armies of Persia had been defeated by the armies of Islam and had lost most of the great Mesopotamian plain. By 642 Islamic armies were in the heartland of Persia. Thus, as the Church of Light began in China, an era of expansion for the Church of the East was coming to an end. It was not long before the church in China was more-or-less cut off from the Mother Church and was able to go its own way theologically and ecclesiastically.

Although the Church of the East differed from the Western Churches in several ways, it played, nevertheless, the same theological game. The Church of the East was hierarchical, liturgical, and doctrinal. It tended to keep to its "old ways" and has even been described as theologically "timid." As we shall see, the Religion of

---

[6] For an excellent synopsis of the history of the Church of the East, see Gillman and Klimkeit, *Christians in Asia Before 1500*, 109-152.

Light, perhaps because of its isolation, broke free in a variety of ways and can hardly be thought of as timid. One of the exciting features of the Religion of Light was its ability to adapt and adopt and, in so doing, to create a whole new theological world-view.

One of Palmer's primary discoveries was that of a tower located about fifty miles from Xian that turns out to be Christian in origin. It seems certain that this Da Qin tower, was a part of a Christian monastery within a larger Daoist complex, one of several Christian establishments that existed during the Tang dynasty in China. The fact that it was located in an area sacred to the Daoists, at the site where Laozi is said to have written the *Dao De Jing*, shows how close the two traditions considered themselves. It was not until 845 C.E. and the persecution of all non-Chinese religions, including especially the Buddhists, that Christianity either withered away or went underground in China.

Besides the tower, with its Christian iconography and its eastward orientation, there is also a great stele in Xian in what is called the Museum of Stone Inscriptions. This is the greatest collection of stone steles in the world. In the midst of the many Confucian steles is one dated 781 C.E. that not only records the essential teachings of the Religion of Light but also provides an account of the official entrance of the faith into China in 635 C.E. as well as subsequent events in the history of the Church. Both the tower and the stele help to explain and are illumined by the cache of Christian documents discovered in 1900 by a Daoist monk named Wang Yuanlu in cave 16 of the Mogao Grottoes, not far from the oasis of Dunhuang in the Gansu desert.[7]

The find was amazing. Some 40,000 scrolls as well as many other relics and artifacts[8] from ancient times came to light. Written in many languages including Tibetan, Uighur, Sogdian as well as Chinese, they included various kinds of records, folk tales and literature and, of course, religious texts. Most of the religious scrolls discovered in these caves were of either Buddhist or Daoist origin, but there were also Christian writings which Palmer designates the "*Jesus Sutras*."[9]

---

[7] For pictures of the interior art work of these caves, see *The Art Treasures of Dunhuang*.

[8] Among the works of art is one fragment of a man with red moustache and beard who is adorned with crosses, an indication that the person was probably Christian. See Whitfield and Farrer, *Caves of the Thousand Buddhas: Chinese art from the Silk Route*, 33.

These were writings apparently used by the Church of Light and represent an unusual blending of Christian, Buddhist, and Daoist ideas. Indeed, early Western translators found them more Daoist than Christian. Unfortunately for scholarship, the discovered scrolls were not protected by the Chinese government but were sold off piecemeal for a fraction of their value or simply stolen. Those that are known to have survived have found homes around the world, from London[10] and Paris to Lanzhou and Japan.

Palmer offers us new translations of eight Christian works from the Mogao caves. Four of these, which he calls sutras, were, he believes, brought to China from elsewhere and translated into Chinese. Then there are four liturgical works written in China in the eighth century, apparently by a Christian monk named Jingjing. These are very important documents for they reveal a great deal about how Christianity adapted itself to the Chinese milieu. There is no guarantee, however, that all of the cache discovered has ever been or ever will be recovered. The question I asked myself is this: Is *Oi Logoi Kruptoi Ye Su* (*The Secret Sayings of Ye Su*) another one of these scrolls that has now come to see the light of day?

Certainly, it must admitted that *The Secret Sayings* is somewhat different in style and content from the others. At the very least, it must be remembered that while all the other religious scrolls were written in Chinese, *The Secret Sayings* is in Greek. Moreover, as we shall see, the content is considerably different as well. Still, there are a number of features which makes *The Secret Sayings* fit quite naturally with the rest.

First of all, all of these documents seek to restate Christianity in Chinese terms. As shall be seen, the *Sayings* is full of references to both Buddhism and early Daoism. Like the first of the *Jesus Sutras*, the *Sayings* often begins with familiar sayings of Jesus from the canonical gospels but interprets them in a new way.

Second, these documents, arising from the Religion of Light, predictably emphasize Jesus as the bringer of light. In the *Sayings*, the resurrection of Ye Su is seen as the revelation of light. Light and water,[11] Chinese embodiments of yang and yin, are the two great images used to portray the essence of Ye Su's teachings,

---

[9] Again, for convenience sake, I shall use his terminology throughout.

[10] For a catalogue of the rich collection of objects from Dunhuang found in the British Museum, see Whitfield and Farrer, *Caves of the Thousand Buddhas: Chinese art from the Silk Route*.

Third, there was, in the Religion of Light, considerable emphasis upon gender equality, a peculiar theme since China was not known for belief in gender equality at all. This is also a major theme of the *Sayings*.

Fourth, and perhaps most important, it is clear that the Religion of Light, unlike the Western Churches, did not prohibit the writing of new gospels which recorded new sayings of Jesus as well as the reinterpretation of old ones. Several works in the collection that Palmer offers do exactly this. So, while the Western Churches settled on a fixed canon and regarded gospels other than Matthew, Mark, Luke and John as inauthentic if not heretical, the Religion of Light continued the early practice of writing gospels to meet new situations.

Thus, although the *Secret Sayings* is unique, many of its characteristics link it to the documents discovered in the caves near Dunhuang. It should also be noted that just as the *Sayings* differs from the *Jesus Sutras*, so, in fact, the *Jesus Sutras* also differ from one another. Therefore, although the use of the Greek language is a problem yet to be resolved, I am drawn to think that the document that I have translated could have been a part of that cache of materials found in the Gansu desert. If not, it still could have been derived from the same period and area. Admittedly, the Greek language remains a stumbling block, but before we tackle that problem we need to explore first what Tang dynasty China was like when Christianity entered and took root.

---

[11] Allen, *The Way of Water and Sprouts of Virtue.*

China Before and During the Tang Dynasty

China Before and During the Tang Dynasty

After the fall of the Han dynasty in 220 C.E. China entered a three hundred fifty year period of division and strife. Although there were moments of unity, as under the Zin, such times were few and did not last. Most of this long period was characterized by a variety of warring states, each claiming to be led by the real Emperor of China. This was also a period when non-Chinese tribes and states, particularly from the north and west, invaded China and established kingdoms. Parts of China were conquered by, and then absorbed, Turkic, Mongolian, Tibetan, and many other ethnic groups. At the same time, the Chinese learned from the various invaders and adopted features of their cultures, including types of food, dress, and religion.

Buddhism

For a number of years, Buddhist monks had been traveling the silk route from India northward, gradually converting the peoples of central Asia. For the most part, it was the Mahayanists who were most successful in this huge area, in large measure because they were willing to adapt to the various cultures they encountered, absorbing into Buddhism the shamanistic and magical practices to which central Asians were accustomed. Therefore, some of the non-Chinese Central Asian invaders who established regimes in China brought with them Buddhist beliefs and made them central for their rule. For instance, it was the Northern Wei dynasty, the To'pa, who constructed the great Buddhist caves-temples at Yungang and then, when they moved their capital, at Lungmen. Although the artistry is impressive, the caves were created, at least in part, to make a political statement about the Buddhist nature of the regime. Particularly in northern China, Buddhism arrived as a political imposition.

In other areas, however, the entrance of Buddhism was less political and more intellectual and spiritual. Buddhism had been known in China during the Han as a foreign religion practiced by traders and diplomats from central Asia and India. With the breakup of the Empire, this Indian faith, which had already become highly sophisticated and multifaceted in India, began to appeal to the Chinese as a way of life to take seriously. This was particularly true because many Chinese, who already had learned something of meditative practice through certain forms of Daoism, found in Buddhist writings much more developed techniques. The first Buddhist writings to be introduced into China, in fact, concerned primarily meditative practice.

As the Chinese began to show interest, more Buddhists from India and Central Asia arrived to meet their intellectual and spiritual needs. Buddhism soon put down roots, building monasteries and offering to China the riches of Buddhist philosophy and practice. There were severe problems, however, for Chinese and Sanskrit are radically different languages and this presented many problems of translation. Often the Chinese did not even have words for what Sanskrit texts were attempting to say. Moreover, Buddhism in India was not one faith but many sects, each with its own sutras and traditions. Although the Chinese were interested in Buddhism, Buddhism itself hardly spoke with one voice. For the Chinese, this was very confusing. Early translations attempted to render Buddhist terms by matching them with terms from Daoist philosophy, a technique (called *ke-yi*) that often turned Buddhism into a kind of crypto-Daoism. Eventually, a distinctive Sino-Buddhist vocabulary, with as many as 2,000 new words and phrases, was developed and translation began in earnest. Among the many translators who made Buddhist thought available to China was the great Kumarajiva (350-?409) who rendered many of the most important Buddhist writings, including the prajna-paramita texts, madyamika philosophic texts, and the Lotus Sutra, into Chinese.

Gradually, the Chinese began to sort through this tremendous mass of materials and arrive at their own conclusions. Many of the best philosophical minds of China during this period wrestled with Buddhist ideas and developed distinctive approaches and institutions that were to dominate the Chinese landscape for centuries. Hui Yuan (334-416), a former Daoist, emphasized the *Sukhavati* (Pure land) Sutras and fostered the development of China's largest and most distinctive Buddhist sect. In a world of great violence and corruption, where hours for peaceful meditation were rare, the *Qing Tu* (Pure Land) sect emphasized that simple faith in the Pure Land of Amitaba is enough to win a place in that Pure Land in the West where enlightenment is very easy to obtain.

Another school that developed during this time was Hua Yen, a sect that emphasized the voluminous and rather mind-boggling Avatamsaka (Garland) sutra. This sutra was taken to be the final summation of the teachings of the Buddha, surpassing all the other sutras that provide only partial truth. For Hua Yen the emphasis is upon unity in plurality, that all is One and One is all. Ultimately, the universe is seen as one bright pearl, the "universal reality of the Buddha."[12]

---

[12] For a good study of Hua Yen, see Cook, *Hua-Yen Buddhism: The Jewel Net of Indra*.

Another similar school that sought to understand all of the sutras through the lens of one, final sutra was founded primarily by Zhi-I (538-597) on Mount Tian-tai located south of Hangzho on the eastern coast of China. The Tian-tai sect (which became Tendai in Japan) emphasized the supreme importance of the Lotus Sutra (*Saddarmapundarikasutra*) as the key to understanding everything else. Part of the appeal of this work is the proclamation that no matter what your status or station or spiritual ability, faith in the Lotus Sutra assures eventual rebirth as a Buddha. Indeed, it would appear that everyone finally will become an Enlightened One.[13]

Still another, most significant tradition to find its roots in this era of violence and warfare was Chan (in Japanese, Zen) Buddhism.[14] According to tradition, Bodhidharma, the founder of Chan arrived in China from India sometime during the first half of the sixth century and eventually settled in Shao-lin, a location not far from the ancient capital of Loyang. Unfortunately, however, whatever information we have about him and his successors is largely found in works like *The Transmission of the Lamp* which read like extended *kong-ans (Zen: koans)*.[15] That is to say, most of what is said is significant spiritually but highly suspect historically. It is not until we get to the beginning of the Tang dynasty and the figure of Hui Neng that we can speak with any historical certainty and even then there are many difficulties.[16] There are, of course, some works that could be by Bodhidharma. In particular, a short text called "The Two Entrances" has been attributed to him by reputable scholars.[17] On the whole, however, the evidence is flimsy and hardly fully convincing.

In any event, as the Tang dynasty began, Buddhism was clearly in flower.[18] There had been attempts by some rulers to curtail or destroy it, but Buddhism proved to

---

[13] For other writings of Tian Tai, see Chappell, ed., *T'ien-T'ai Buddhism: An Outline of the Fourfold Teachings.*

[14] Among the many books about Chan (Zen) are Heinrich Dumolin, *Zen Buddhism: A History, Volume I, China and India.* and John C.H. Wu, *The Golden Age of Zen.*

[15] *Koans* are paradoxical, mind wrenching stories used for meditation. Many are about early Chan Masters.

[16] See *The Platform Sutra of the Sixth Patriarch.*.

[17] Jeffrey L. Broughton, *The Bodhidharma Anthology*, 9-12. See also Red Pine, *The Zen Teaching of Bodhidharma*, 3-7.

[18] For a good placing of Buddhism within the historical developments of the Tang, see Stanley Weinstein, *Buddhism Under the T"ang*

be too popular among the people and the intellectuals to be easily done away with. Almost invariably, the rulers were forced to back off and leave the monasteries alone. Buddhism, by the beginning of the Tang, had already developed the afore-mentioned and several other smaller indigenous Chinese sects, a rich artistic tradition manifested for us particularly in cave art, and a philosophical tradition elaborated from Indian roots which was to sustain Buddhism during long centuries of both persecution and growth. It had become the predominant religion of the Middle Kingdom.

The Indigenous Traditions

The indigenous Chinese religious traditions, known in the West as Confucianism and Daoism, had also changed and developed greatly during the period of discord after the Han and before the Tang. Whether Confucianism is a religion at all is a matter of some debate. Perhaps one should just say it is simply a tradition of political and social values and structures made manifest in government, in the family, and in education. Although this tradition had little to teach theologically, it did frequently sponsor rites and rituals that it regarded as important for a strong society.

The break-up of the Han fostered a general lack of confidence in Confucianism as the ideology to unite China. Intellectuals turned either to the study of Buddhist philosophy or to *xuan xue* (mysterious learning), a philosophical movement which returned for inspiration to the Daoist classics and the *I Jing*, a Confucian work which could be used for metaphysical purposes.[19] As a consequence, the other Confucian classics went largely unstudied for several generations.[20] Commentators on them from this era are few and far between.

Although the fall of the Empire made it impossible for there to be one unified set of Imperial rites, Confucian rituals employed in connection with the Imperial Court did not fall into total disuse. In fact, the long period of disunity was a time when many rituals were standardized.[21] The system of higher education so

---

[19] Jacques Gernet, *A History of Chinese Civilization*, 2nd Ed.), 206.

[20] *Ibid.*, 203ff.

[21] Thomas Wilson, "Sacrifice and the Imperial Cult of Confucius," *History of Religions* 41.3 (Feb. 2002), 262.

important in the Han, however, did, for the most part, collapse.[22] Although Confucian academies continued to operate, the big university simply ceased to function and, because it failed to operate, social status replaced intellectual merit as the grounds for appointment and advancement.[23] Confucianism remained as a set of implicit family and societal values and as a set of ritual functions to be performed, but until the revival of the empire seems to have remained largely dormant intellectually. With the Tang, however, Confucianism began to make a comeback and gradually resumed its role as the educator of China.

Daoism, the other great Chinese tradition, is even more difficult to define or conceptualize. There is a philosophical tradition embodied in several great classics such as the *Dao De Jing, Zhuangzi, Wenzi, Huainanzi,* and *Liezi* that are often referred to by the various sects of the tradition. At the same time, Daoism is neither the creation of the philosophers nor is it a consistent whole, for it embodies magical practices, healing cults, experimental alchemy and belief in a great plethora of gods and goddesses, spirits and dark forces. In some respects, it cannot be separated from Chinese folk religion and its shamanistic roots. In many writings about the history of Chinese religion, everything that is not Confucian or Buddhist tends to be thrown, with at least partial justification, into a great pot called Daoism.

Before the decline of the Han, such Daoism seemed to have little organization or structure at all. The most acute non-Confucian philosopher, the illiterate hermit on some sacred mountain, the local shamanic healer, the alchemist looking for some elixir that would bring immortality, all are lumped together as Daoists. With the faltering of the Han in the second century, however, came the Daoist search for renewal and order. In fact, the Han was, in large measure brought an end by Daoist movements: the Yellow Turbans of east and central China and *Tianshi Dao* (Way of the Celestial Masters)[24] that began in Sichuan in the west. The former became a revolutionary movement that actually fought the imperial armies. Eventually the Yellow Turbans were defeated, but the imperial power was

---

[22] The imperially sponsored university (*daxue*) was begun in 124 B.C. By the reign of Shun Ti (125-144) it had grown to an institution of 30,000 students. Twitchett and Loewe, *The Ch'in and Han Empire,s* Vol. I of *The Cambridge History of China,* 756-757.

[23] Twichett, ed. *Sui and T'ang China, 589-906.*Part *I,* Vol. 3 of *The Cambridge History of China,* 90.

[24] Because participants were assessed five pecks of rice, the movement was called derisively *Wudoumi Dao* (the Way of the five pecks of rice).

so weakened by the conflict that the government soon collapsed. The *Tianshi Dao* (known derisively as the Way of the Five Pecks of Rice), which was founded by Zhang Daoling, developed over time a rather militaristic structure and even came to set up a theocratic state in Su in northern Sichuan. It became, indeed, the first really organized form of Daoism with a hierarchy of priests, well-developed rituals, and spiritual teachings.

This religious organization, led by the Celestial Masters, emphasized the *Dao De Jing* as the leaders understood it, embryonic breathing techniques, and various rituals of confession and atonement. The Masters also sought to distance themselves from folk religion and developed a distinctive set of teachings that set them apart from ordinary Chinese temple cults. For a time, the movement was established as a state religion in part of Sichuan but by the sixth century it had lost its impetus. It survived, however, and then was revived somewhat in the eighth century. Although ranked as the lowest of the Daoist sects during the Tang, it outlived most of its rivals and endures today as one of the main Daoist sects. During the Tang, however, it was of minor importance and hence we will not describe it further.

Another Daoist tradition to survive the death of the Han dynasty was that of the alchemist that, during the Han, had produced so many quests for the elixir of immortality. Ge Hong (280-340), in his *Nei Pian*, presents us with a collection of writings about many facets of that tradition.[25] The author himself was not so much of an innovator as a preserver of tradition. Lying side-by-side in the collection are a variety of alchemical formulas, essays on theology, and advice on how to enter a forest possessed by demonic spirits. This tradition was to continue in the Tang as Daoist alchemists searched for the elixir that would make the body immortal. It is likely that Emperor Wu Zong, who is best known for presiding over the closing of Buddhist monasteries in 842-845 C.E., died from imbibing elixirs prepared by the alchemists.

Along side the Celestial Master School and the alchemists there developed two other schools of Daoist thought. The first to be mentioned is the *shangqing* (Highest Purity) movement. This school of thought was initiated in the fourth century when one Yang Xi began to receive secret texts at night from the gods and spirits. These texts, which were written in good literary style and with beautiful calligraphy, then became the basis for a whole new movement in Daoism.

---

[25] Ware, trans., *Alchemy, Medicine, and Religion in China of A.D. 320: The Nei P'ien of Ko Hung.*

The *shangqing*, unlike the Celestial Masters, adopted no military style organization. There seems to have been much less emphasis upon corporate, public rituals and organized structure, though there was a kind of spiritual hierarchy culminating in a patriarch. The secret texts were passed on from a Master to a student who was ready to receive them. As Isabelle Robinet says,

> Above all else, the disciple swore never to reveal the text without good cause. The text could be transmitted only to those worthy to receive it, those whose names were inscribed in the celestial registers and who possessed "jade bones," made of the incorruptible and precious substance that forms the body of the immortal. In short, the texts could be passed only to those predestined for immortality.[26]

The secrets in these texts, whose numbers increased over the years, are much too complex to discuss here, but it should be said that they involve teaching the techniques of visualization through which various deities and powers can be made manifest in the human body.[27] Sometimes they employ the ingredients of what came to be called *neidan* or internal alchemy. That is to say, the external quest by alchemy for the elixir of immortality was internalized and visualized. Thus the *shangqing* school foreshadowed the Complete Reality school of Daoism which was to develop in China during the Song dynasty.[28]

Shangqing, in any event, was in ascendance during the Tang period and would undoubtedly have been known about by members of the Religion of Light. Perhaps the insistence upon secrecy, so important in *Oi Logoi Kruptoi Ye Su* was influenced by the *shangqing*. Whether the *Secret Sayings* was also read employing the techniques of visualization, can only be a matter of speculation.

The second Daoist school particularly active during the Tang followed the *shangqing* tradition both temporally and textually. The *lingbao* tradition claimed to begin in the third century, but, in fact, started at the beginning of the fifth. In many ways, it was inspired by its predecessor, also offering texts revealed by the

---

[26] Robinet, *Taoism: Growth of a Religion*, 127.

[27] For an example of such a text and how the user employed visualization, see E.H. Schafer, The Jade Woman of Great Mystery," *History of Religions* 17 (1978): 387-98.

[28] For a good example of an internal alchemy text, see Cleary, trans. *Understanding Reality: A Taoist Alchemical Classic by Chang Po-Tuan.*

gods. *Lingbao* is usually translated "sacred jewel," but could equally well be translated as "spiritual treasure." What it offers as its treasure is a mixture of several traditions, including the Buddhist. The *shangqing* school sometimes alluded to Buddhism, but the *lingbao* not only overtly borrowed certain conceptions like salvation, which were not indigenous to China, but also used transliterated Sanskrit names for heavens and deities, etc. Some of the revealed texts were also available through other non-revealed sources; some of the texts were rather crude in formulation and expression. Nevertheless, the school attracted many followers.

One of the reasons, one may suppose, is that *lingbao*, unlike *shangqing*, drew from the traditions of the Celestial Masters and developed impressive public rituals. These rituals, in fact, became the source for Daoist rituals of the present day. De-emphasized are the techniques of visualization and the individual and solitary search for purification and renewal. Instead, the new texts (which actually include some from the *shangqing*) are more public. Confucian values are given their place; so is the Buddhist emphasis upon compassion and the salvation of all creatures. In other words, *The lingbao* tradition is highly syncretic with something for everyone.[29]

This general tendency toward syncretism was to continue during the Tang. As a sometimes-established state religion, Daoism sought to bring together its different schools, form a canon of its authoritative writings, and develop an ideology comparable to that of the Buddhists. Centripetal forces led to the adoption of both Confucian and Buddhist ideas while centrifugal forms pushed Daoism to develop its own unique identity.

The Sui and the Tang

In 590 C.E., after centuries of disunity, Yang Zhien (541-604) was able to unite China under his control and found the short-lived Sui dynasty. Before the dynasty came to an end, he and his son, who succeeded him, were able to extend the Empire to Taiwan and into the Turkic regions of the west. Unfortunately for the Emperor, his military adventures did not go well in Korea and China failed in that area of expansion. Moreover, so much money was spent on wars and public service projects such as canals and so many people were conscripted to do the

---

[29] For translations of *shangqing* and *lingbao* texts, see Bokenkamp, *Early Daoist Scriptures*.

work that public dissatisfaction grew enormously. Consequently, Yang Guang, Yang Zhien's son and successor, was assassinated and a whole new dynasty came to power. One of the most glorious eras in the history of China was about to begin, The Tang era was initiated in 618 C.E. and lasted until 906. During this time China became probably the largest and strongest empire on earth and Chinese culture, in this context, blossomed.

According to the great stele in Xian, it was in 635, just seventeen years after the founding of the Tang dynasty that Aluoben, a bishop of the Church of the East, entered China from the west and was greeted by Emperor Tang Taizong. Bishop Aluoben, had apparently made the long journey from his home in Persia with the specific purpose of introducing what was to be called the Religion of Light into China. He came with an entourage and scriptures that he presented for the Emperor's inspection. Clearly, the whole affair was thoroughly prepared and, like all well-planned diplomatic events, came as no surprise to anyone. The stele then tells us that after these documents were translated and read by the Emperor, he issued a proclamation welcoming the message of the Church as "mysterious and wonderful beyond our understanding."[30] Thus the Emperor allowed the faith to take root and grow in the Middle Kingdom. The history of Christianity in China had begun.

What was it like in this new world? The first thing to be said is that although the Tang dynasty marks one of the greatest eras in Chinese history, it was not without its violence, its tensions, and its controversy. The Tang, which began with revolt and assassinations did not bring a perfect peace. In the east and south there were many who resented the fact that the capital, which was supposed to unite all China, was located in the west, in Chang-an, at the terminus of the silk route. Some may have resented that the Li family that founded the dynasty was, in fact, partly Turkic and that the capital city seemed to be overrun with every sort of for- eigner from Persia, Uzbekistan, India, Tibet, etc. Some may have been concerned that Emperor Tang Taizong, to win the throne, had actually killed the crown prince and other brothers and had forced his father, the founder of the dynasty, into retirement.

At the same time, China's northern and western neighbors always eyed the rich lands of China with greed and envy and were especially anxious to win back from

---

[30] Palmer, *op. cit.*, 227.

China those territories along the silk route that had once been theirs. Soon, too, Arab armies would be pressing eastward, ready to conquer and convert in the name of Allah. By the eighth century, one of the central questions was: who would control those vast regions of Central Asia, the Middle Kingdom or the armies of Islam? A great battle, fought against far away Tashkent in 751 C.E., was to render historical judgment against the Chinese and open Central Asia to Islam. It was, indeed, one of the turning points in world history.

The Tang era was marked not only by repeated clashes with external enemies but also by occasional insurrections within. In 690 C.E., for instance, a former concubine of Emperor Tang Taizong who had become concubine and then wife of his successor, deposed, upon her husband's death, the rightful heir and made herself Empress. Thus, for several years the Tang dynasty, in fact, came to an end. Empress Wu won the favor of the eastern gentry by moving the capital to Loyang and of the Buddhist establishment by contributing to the *Sangha* huge sums of money. By 713, however, the tide had turned. External pressure from the Turks, internal plots and counter plots, and the death of Empress Wu weakened the government. Empress Wei, the successor, was assassinated and the Tang came back to power in the person of Emperor Xuanzong. He ruled for some forty-two years, producing the second great cultural flowering of the Tang. Shortly after his death, the insurrection by An Lu-shan in the mid-eighth century again momentarily ended the Tang, as the rebel defeated the imperial armies and actually declared himself Emperor. Only the help of the Uighurs, a neighboring Central Asian tribe, and the assassination of An Lu-shan by one of the eunuchs in the palace saved the Tang from disaster.

During the Tang, there were also the machinations of the various religious groups who sought imperial favor and power. Despite their religious stance against desire and their strong assertion of the virtue of compassion, the Buddhists were quite capable of amassing great wealth in their monasteries, enslaving thousands to work their fields, and garnering political support whenever and wherever they could.

Daoists, in their turn, though smaller in numbers and generally less politically powerful, nevertheless worked to oust the Buddhists from their dominant role in society and government. This struggle between the Buddhists and Daoists began full force in the reign of the first major Tang ruler, Tang Taizong. The Emperor, whose name before assuming the throne was Li Shih-min, was of partly Turkic stock. His mother was Turkic in origin and devoutly Buddhist. Although she died when Li Shih-min was quite young, she seems to have had a profound influence on him. From the beginning of his reign he, quite unlike his rather anti-Buddhist father, gave to the Buddhists memorials, temples and other benefits.

In 637 C.E., just two years after the Christian embassy arrived, the Daoists convinced the Emperor that he, as a Li, was a descendant of the famous culture hero and philosopher Laozi. This "fact" was of particular importance for the Emperor because it helped to justify his position as ruler over the Chinese. Those who disliked his Turkic origins now had to contend with his auspicious Chinese genealogy. As a result, the Emperor proclaimed that the Daoists should take precedence over the Buddhists in ritual matters. The Buddhists, of course, were miffed and responded that the so-called Daoists did not really follow Laozi at all, and therefore should not benefit from the esteemed Emperors lineage.[31] Nevertheless, the Daoists convinced the Emperor with this genealogical fiction and from time to time, at least, wielded power. When they did so, Buddhists tended to suffer.

Sometimes, of course, Daoists and Buddhists existed side-by-side without enmity. This certainly happened on Mount Tian-Tai where the Tian Tai monks lived peaceably next to a Daoist monastery. Nevertheless, there were always Daoists seeking some advantage, even arguing that after Laozi left China he went to India and taught the Buddha what he knew. Eventually, in the mid-ninth century, the Emperor Wu Zong, who was a Daoist devotee who keenly resented the power of the Buddhists, accepted all those Daoist arguments and confiscated the vast Buddhist properties. The fact that the Emperor was strapped for funds also encouraged him in his campaign. He melted down the numerous bronze Buddhas to mint coins, and returned thousands of *bhikkus* and *bhikkunis* to lay life. A Japanese Buddhist monk by the name of Ennin recorded this whole terrible chapter in Chinese religious history in his diary and is a wonderful source for knowledge of the period.[32]

After the disaster of 842-45 C.E., when Buddhism and other foreign religions were attacked and thousands of monks returned to lay life, Buddhism was offered some reprive. Under the next emperor, Xunzong, many monasteries and temples were reopened and Buddhism reemerged, but soon a civil war broke out which was to ravage the country severely. In some ways, this revolution did even more damage than the persecution under Emperor Wu. As a result, Buddhism in

---

[31] For an interesting account of Tang Taizong's attitudes, see Wright, "T'ang T'ai-tsung and Buddhism.".

[32] Ennin, *Diary; the Record of a Pilgrimage to China in Search of the Law.*

China was never the same again. Monastic libraries were been destroyed. Therefore sects like Tian-tai and Hua Yen that depended upon texts were severely hurt. Many smaller sects never recovered and even the largest, such as the *Qing Tu*, remained at diminished strength. Nevertheless, it was the sects that emphasized personal experience rather than textual study that were to endure. Thus, Buddhism in China became largely Qing Tu and Chan. One further result was that while several sects died in China, Japanese monks returned home and preserved there what had been destroyed, or for the most part destroyed, on the mainland. Thus Tian-Tai Buddhism largely disappeared in China, but continued in Japan as Tendai, eventually spawning other movements such as Nichiren Buddhism and even Sokka Gakkai.

All this means that the followers of the Religion of Light were observers of an often quite nasty struggle for power between two groups that both theoretically attacked attachment to the world and the desire for ego enhancement. This may very well have inspired the sayings of Ye Su that deplore the organization of religion and the establishment of the church. It may also lie behind the saying that although all religions are based upon the light, they are all subject to corruption. In any event, what for a long time was a struggle between Daoism and Buddhism eventually turned on the Religion of Light as well, for in 845 C.E. all the foreign religious establishments were closed and Christianity, except for, perhaps, some hidden, underground movements, disappeared.

Despite all the violence and controversy that characterized the age, this was a wonderful time to be in China. Chang-an,[33] the capital, was a modern city laid out in a grid pattern with broad avenues and streets. Imperial buildings were lavish; glorious temples and shrines were around every corner. Although, during the Sui, the area around Chang-an was still depopulated by famine and war, when the city reached its zenith under the Tang, it had a population of more than 2,000,000 people. In that great city one could find Confucian literati deeply steeped in the intellectual traditions of the past and Manicheans from the Uighurs who followed the dualistic religion of Mani. There were Zoroastrians from Persia who built fire temples and shamans from the Central Asian steppes. Buddhists of all sorts flocked to the capital and built their temples throughout the city. There were Daoist alchemists offering elixirs of immortality and, in the hills nearby, Daoist hermits seeking refuge from the world. There were merchants

---

[33] Chang-An means "long peace." Its modern day counterpart is Xian or western peace.

from India and embassies from far away Byzantium.[34] Chang-an was a Chinese city, but it was also a microcosm of the world.

Among the exciting developments during the Tang for anyone interested in the spiritual life was the growth of Chan Buddhism and its most unusual approach to the teachings. For Chan, what Buddhism offers is not myths or doctrines or promises of future rewards. Rather, Chan Buddhism offers a spiritual transformation that is communicated from Mind to Mind, "outside the Scriptures." Although the roots of Chan are to be found in works like the Lankavantara Sutra,[35] Chan itself claimed no interest in learning from books. Instead it is the immediate experience, the slap or blow or peculiarly paradoxical story that leads to that transformation called enlightenment. One story will have to suffice to illustrate:

> The Master ascended the hall. A monk asked, "What is the mean-ing of basic Buddhism?"
> The Master held his flywhisk straight up.
> The monk gave a shout.
> The Master struck him.[36]

Hui-Neng (638-713), the first of the Chan Masters that we can know at all his-torically, was not yet born when the Religion of Light arrived officially in China. Therefore, since the author of the *Secret Sayings* seems to show more affinity to Chan than any other form of Buddhism, it is likely that he or she arrived on the scene somewhat later, perhaps during the illustrious reign of Xuanzong. If that is the case, our author would have been a contemporary of such famous Tang poets as Li Bo (701-762), Du Fu (712-770), and Wang Wei (699-759?). If, however, he lived in the early ninth century he could have witnessed the bringing of the Buddha's tooth to the capital by the Buddhists and perhaps read Han Yu's sting-ing rebuke of such superstition. Among the great poets of that age was Bo Zhu-I (772-846). In the ninth century our author could also have known such Chan notables as Huang Po (d. 850), Zhao Zhou (778-?) Dung Shan (807-869) and Lin Zhi (d. 866).

---

[34] Such an embassy arrive in 643 C.E. Was our author among the delegation?
[35] D.T. Suzuki, *Studies in the Lankavatara Sutra.*
[36] Lin Chi, *The Zen Teachings of Master Lin-Chi*, 15.

It may be a mistake, however, to try to relate the author of *The Secret Sayings* too closely to the development of Chan. What constitutes the similarities between them is largely what they share in common with Daoism. In *The Secret Sayings* there are no hints of "wall gazing" or of the paradoxical story and saying which so marks Chan's expression. There are no slaps, no punches. The Source may be unspeakable, but the author finds much that is still possible to say that is not an impenetrable paradox.

When Aluoben came to China in 635 he undoubtedly stopped at the oasis in Dunhuang and could very well have visited the famous Mogao caves, already finely decorated with a Buddhist art strongly under the influence of Central Asian styles. By the eighth century, however, new caves had been covered with far more Chinese artistry. A traveler from the west would have seen the great, more than life-size, painted clay statues of the Buddhas, Bodhisattvas, and arhats set within grottoes covered by designs and figures. The Mogao Grottoes brought Chinese art to a very high level of maturity and contain the finest examples of Tang religious art.

Although most of the Tang art outside these grottoes has long since been destroyed, the age of Tang was noted for its artists. Nothing by the famous Wu Dao-Zi remains, but we can appreciate something of the artistic grandeur of the times by viewing works attributed to Wang Wei (699-759), Zhang Xuan (8th C.), and Zhou Fang (8th C.) While the art of Mogao is obviously Buddhist, these other artists painted scenes from ordinary life that show less interest in the other-worldly Paradise of Amitabha and more in how actual people lived. Certainly the fine porcelain produced during this period also expresses the wonderfully aes-thetic sense of a people who enjoyed life and loved beauty. From all these rem-nants of a richly artistic era we can reconstruct a fairly clear picture of how the Tang Chinese lived.

Having set the stage for the Religion of Light, it is now time to look more care-fully at those few remnants of that movement left to us in the so-called *Jesus Sutras* and the great stele of Xian.

The Sutras of the Religion of Light

The Sutras of the Religion of Light

Because textual evidence is so meager, it is difficult to tell how representative the texts from the Religion of Light discovered in the Mogao Caves really are. Did these works supplement the canonical gospels and other Christian writings from antiquity or did they essentially replace them? Do these represent the Church's position or are they idiosyncratic documents that represent only individual opinions? Did the Church remain largely a community of aliens living in China or did it become thoroughly Chinese? None of these questions can be adequately answered at this time. The best we can do is look at the writings themselves to discover what they reveal about the Religion of Light and its believers.

It is probable that the first so-called sutra, "The Sutra of the Teaching of the World-Honored One"[37] was brought to China from Persia and illustrates how Buddhism may have affected the church even before it arrived in the Middle Kingdom. Essentially, it is a garbled retelling of the basic gospel story. It is full of quotations and paraphrases from gospels, particularly from the Sermon on the Mount. The word "God" is not used. Instead, the text refers either to the "World Honored One" or to "One Sacred Spirit."

The Messiah in this Gospel does die, but not particularly to forgive the sins of humanity. Instead the text says that in dying "He showed the holy transformation beyond all previous reckoning."[38] Although this author makes the resurrection seem a bit more historical than in the *Secret Sayings* and does promise that the Messiah has opened the gates of heaven so that those who believe will be raised from the "Yellow Springs" after death,[39] the emphasis upon transformation links the *Secret Sayings* and this sutra closely together. Indeed, in both form and content, they seem quite similar.

There are several references to Buddhism as in the mention of the Five Attributes[40] that are undoubtedly the five *skandha*[41]. The reference to qi[42] is also

---

[37] Palmer, *op. cit.*, 60-69.

[38] *Ibid.*, 63.

[39] *Ibid.*

[40] *Ibid.*

[41] According to Buddhism the self is made up of five skandhas: body, sensation, perception, ideation, and consciousness. At death, these separate. The self, therefore, no longer exists.

[42] *Ibid.*, 66.

reminiscent of Daoism. It is difficult to know, however, whether these references to Chinese traditions were in the original manuscript or were added later by the person who translated the text into Chinese. Certainly, none of these references is as integral to the text as the references that are in the *Secret Sayings.*

The Second Sutra, "The Sutra of Cause, Effect, and Salvation"[43] is also thought to have been brought to China from elsewhere, but it is of quite a different order. Rather than being a paraphrase of the gospels, it is a far more philosophical piece, addressing the question of creation and the relation of soul to body. It discusses the Sacred Spirit as the key to the good life and the dangers of the evil spirits and ghosts who try to tempt us and lead us astray. The Messiah is mentioned, but only briefly. The word God appears, but, on the whole, the Ultimate is conceived at existing "beyond" personality.

This treatment of human existence and its source shows the obvious influence of Buddhist thought. The five *skandhas* are emphasized as are the notions of reincarnation and karma. Everything in the text is recast so that basic Christianity—and it is quite basic—addresses the questions that popular Buddhism raises. Nothing of the sophistication of *Madhyamika* or *Yogacharya* philosophy is found here. From a systematic point of view there seem to be many loose ends. Still the attempt to unite the Christian message and Chinese thought is parallel to, if less sophisticated than, the *Secret Sayings.*

The Third Sutra, "The Sutra of Origins"[44] is said by Martin Palmer to be less sophisticated than the Second Sutra, and so, perhaps, it is. I would suggest, however, that it is a straightforward attempt to equate the One Sacred Spirit of Christianity and the Dao of Daoism. In this work, the One Sacred Spirit turns out to be the root of everything, the Void from which all flows. It operates according to the ancient principle of *wei wu wei,* action through no action. It does nothing, yet through it everything is accomplished. Like a hidden archer, it cannot be seen or known, but its effects, like the arrow in flight, presuppose its existence. The One Sacred Spirit is what keeps Heaven from falling; it is the explanation for what is.

Although it is conceivable that this sutra was written elsewhere, it seems to me that it is so in tune with basic Daoism that it is more likely that it was composed

---

[43] *Ibid.,* 139-146.
[44] *Ibid.,* 147-150.

in China, for the Chinese. There is in this work, in fact, little that shows a definite connection to the Bible. It is truly Daoism behind a very thin veil.

The Fourth Sutra, "The Sutra of Jesus Christ"[45] combines many of the attributes of the other sutras. It begins by emphasizing that God is unknowable, like the wind that cannot be seen but nevertheless has profound effects. The Messiah, however, has come to teach us the law, the precepts, through which we can know God. Only the righteous can "see" God. Therefore, living a righteous life is essential. The work then proceeds to set forth the rules for life that, in part, turn out to be the Ten Commandments with extra emphasis upon honoring your parents and the Emperor. The deference to Confucianism is clear. Then the text goes on to say that these laws are not enough, now listing many other actions that are important to achieve righteousness. Many of these precepts come right out of the gospels. The ethic offered, then, is a combination of ideas from the Old and New Testaments. There is, however, no sense of the inevitability of sin due to the fallen nature of humanity. The message is clearly one that St. Augustine would have deplored.

The last part of the work is a retelling of parts of the gospel story. In particular, the text offers versions of the incarnation, baptism, and crucifixion of Ye Su who comes primarily to teach humans what righteousness is. His death and resurrection are a proof that he comes from the "Cool Breeze" but seems to have little to do with forgiveness. The gospel has become a series of lessons in morality. Although it begins with the Buddhas and Bodhisattvas showing reverence by circumambulating the Messiah, there are fewer evidences of Chinese concepts in this work. Like the first sutra, therefore, it could easily have been written elsewhere and simply have been translated for a Chinese audience.

Beside these four Sutras, there are four other liturgical texts that date from the eighth century. At least three of them seem to be by Jingjing, a monk apparently well known for his literary talents. His name, in fact, appears on the Great Stele and was probably the author of that text too.[46]

---

[45] *Ibid.*, 159-168.

[46] According to S. H. Moffett, Jingjing also collaborated with Prajna, a Buddhist monk in the translation of a Buddhist text. This collaboration would have brought him in contact with both Kukai, the founder of Japanese Shingon, and Saicho, the founder of Tendai in Japan. See Moffett, *A History of Christianity in Asia*, Vol. I: Beginnings to 1500, 301-302.

The first of these Liturgical Sutras, the "Da Qin/Syrian Christian liturgy of taking Refuge in the Three" is dated in 720 and was, it seems, from a Christian monastery in Gansu, perhaps in Dunhuang. Martin Palmer has arranged it liturgically, alternating priest and congregation, though this is not in the original text. The notion of taking refuge as well as the mention of Dharma Lords, the Ocean of Dharma, and the Heavenly Wheel all indicate the influence of Buddhism. Referring to God as the Jade-faced One and to our "Original nature" sounds much more Daoist, though these could also be from Buddhism. Mention of God as Allaha (a Syriac version of the Hebrew Elohim) and the reference to singing to God sounds far more Syriac and Western.

The second Liturgical Sutra,[47] is a rather short work in praise of the Trinity, the saints (who are here called Dharma Kings), and the Sutras, some of which have been discussed above. Some of the Dharma Kings, like the four gospel writers, Moses, David, and Paul are well known to western readers. Most of the others are not. It seems noteworthy that among the texts to be praised nothing from the Bible itself is included. The list of texts also reminds us that many of the central texts of the movement are still unavailable to us. Whether they were originally among the scrolls found in the Mogao Caves is, of course, a matter of speculation.

The third of these Liturgical Sutras[48] is by far the longest and most complex. Although, of course, it could be chanted, it seems far less liturgical than the others in this group.

Essentially, it is a discourse by the Messiah with some leading questions offered by disciples, The whole discourse, which contains few quotations from the Bible, is permeated by Daoist and Buddhist ideas. The Messiah's teachings are summarized by four rules: "no wanting, no doing, no piousness, no truth."[49] It is interesting that these are exactly the themes of Ye Su in the *Secret Sayings*. No wanting, of course, implies no craving, for it is craving which prevents us from finding inner peace. The theme of "no doing' reflects the Daoist teaching of *wei wu wei*, and means to "act without action." The point is to live naturally, without trying to be something you are not. It is to go, as the modern saying puts it, "with the flow."

---

[47] Palmer, *op. cit.*,183-185.
[48] *Ibid.*, 189-201.
[49] *Ibid.*, 192, 198-200.

The teaching of "no piousness" is directly reflected in the *Secret Sayings* and, for that matter, in the Bible. What it means is that one should never let piety show, for piety seen by others soon becomes a matter of pride. This theme is quite consistent with Jesus' repeated attacks upon the hypocrites and his commands to keep one's prayer life secret.

The teaching of "no truth" may seem surprising, for religions are supposed to teach the truth. That, however, is seen as the problem with religions. The sutra emphasizes not judging, not insisting upon one's way, treating everyone equally. Religious truth, as it is normally conceived, is seen as a barrier to mutual understanding rather than as a unifying force.

This way of life, says the Messiah, promotes peace and happiness in a world in which everyone seems to be craving for something, whether it be power or sex or amusement or the truth, but in which everyone eventually dies and must relinquish all for which they craved. The Religion of Light provides the armor to wear in this world of suffering and will bring all who follow it to the other shore of Peace. As can be seen, the *Secret Sayings* in many ways offers a very similar path.

The fourth Liturgical Sutra is entitled "The Christian Liturgy in Praise of the Three Sacred Powers"[50] and may be a translation/interpretation of the famous hymn known in Latin as "Gloria in Excelsis Deo." It is written to glorify the Trinity: the Compassionate Father, Radiant Son, and Pure Wind King. Nevertheless, there are also many Chinese touches which add different dimensions to its meaning. In particular, there is special emphasis upon God's unseen, unchanging, and dazzling nature. God is the root and essence of all. Although God's Love is mentioned, the deity seems very much like the Dao of the Daoists. On the whole, however, the theology of the poem is closer to that of Western Christianity than many of the other texts.

The last of the documents[51] from the Religion of Light available to us comes not from the Mogao Caves but is found on that great stele originally erected in 781 when the Da Qin monastery constructed its pagoda. It is particularly significant because this document contains an official statement of the faith of the Religion of Light[52] and therefore is unlikely to be the result of some idiosyncratic thinker.

---

50 *Ibid.*, 202-204.
51 *Ibid.*, 224-232.
52 *Ibid.*, 224-232.

The Stele begins with a brief synopsis of Religion of Light belief, with a description of how the world began. Unlike the Bible, it speaks of the beginning as a primordial void out of which emerged the Most High Lord who is named Joshua (which here is seen as the real name of Ye Su). Joshua not only encompasses the three subtle and wondrous bodies but actually died on a cross to save humanity.

Humans, the appointed guardians of all creation, were born with pure natures, but lost them when Satan tempted them with "glitter and gold." Thus the central problem of humans is desire. Ye Su is born into the world from a virgin in order, through his teachings, to restore to human beings to their original purity. The text says:

> We use abstinence to subdue thoughts of desire; and we use stillness to build our foundation. At seven we gather for service to pray for the salvation of all. Every seven days we have an audience with heaven. We purify our hearts and return to the simple and natural way of truth. This truth cannot be named but its function surpasses all expectations. When forced to give it a name, we call it the Religion of Light, As it is with the Way, that which is sacred is not sacred unless it is highly sacred, and that which is the Way is not the Way unless it is the Great Way.[53]

Part III of the Stele tells the story of how Aluoben came to China in 635, how the faith was approved by the Emperor, and how the Da Qing Monastery was first built in the capital city. What follows is a synopsis of how various Emperors approved of and aided the Religion of Light and how it spread around the Empire. It mentions some trouble with the Buddhists, but essentially this is a very positive report about the fortunes of the Church in the Middle Kingdom. Because steles are always basically propagandistic there is no way to tell from this document just how large the church became, whether it ever really attracted many Chinese, and whether the emperors were really as positive and helpful as the stele suggests.

In any event, it is clear that the Religion of Light was an institution that adapted rapidly to its new milieu and, in fact, transformed itself under the influence of Chinese thought. The active, personal God of the Bible is replaced by the great, unseen Emptiness that manifests itself in the world as Spirit or Wind. Ye Su (Jesus) still dies for humanity, but to teach the Way rather than to forgive. And

---

[53] *Ibid.*, 226.

the Way, far from being elaborated in intellectual doctrines, now is a way of sub-dued desire, simplicity, and silence. Emphasis throughout is upon the ethical and spiritual teachings of Jesus and not the theology of Paul. There is little mention of church hierarchy, for all people are to be seen as equal, nor of the Eucharist, the central liturgical element in Christian worship. Rather, every seven days the believers have an audience with Heaven, an audience, I suppose, in which they listen more than they speak. There seems to be little interest in eschatology. Primary emphasis is upon the transformation of the self through the muting of desire.

Having had this brief glimpse into the Religion of Light, let us now turn to the *Secret Sayings of Ye Su* to see if and how this work also adopts Buddhist and Daoist ideas. Does this document also fit into this era of the Tang dynasty when the Religion of Light was accommodating itself to the culture of the Middle Kingdom and thereby thriving?

Buddhist and Daoist Concepts in The Secret Sayings

Buddhist and Daoist Concepts in the *Secret Sayings*

Buddhist Concepts

The Secret Sayings of Ye Su contains obvious indications that it was influenced by both Buddhist and Daoist thought. Many of Ye Su's sayings recorded here bear direct resemblance to what is taught in the canonical gospels, but the focus and context have now changed. Most particularly, the author has accepted as essential the Buddha's diagnosis of the human predicament. That is, human life has become corrupted by desire and that desire is rooted in a false sense of self. Han Shan, the great hermit poet of the later Tang, put it this way:

> Man, living in the dust,
> Is like a bug trapped in a bowl,
> All day he scrabbles round and round,
> But never escapes from the bowl that holds him.
> The immortals are beyond his reach,
> His cravings have no end,
> While months and years flow by like a river
> Until, in an instant, he has grown old.[54]

As we have seen, this emphasis upon egotism as the source of human woe is found in the *Jesus Sutras*. The very first saying of *The Secret Sayings* also sets forth the same idea as the basic premise of the whole collection:

To the multitude I speak only in parables, for the world is drunk with its own importance, addicted to its own pride. Drunken understanding is worse than drunken ignorance.

The notion that Jesus speaks only in parables to the multitude is, of course, found in Mark 4:11, but now Ye Su provides a new reason. The world is inebriated, addicted to the ego. Therefore, as long as this egotism, which expresses itself in craving, prevails, Ye Su's message will be misinterpreted. Moreover, the gospel, interpreted egotistically, constitutes a severe danger.

---

54 Han Shan, *Cold Mountain: 100 poems by the T'ang poet Han-shan*, 98.

The idea of the world being inebriated by desire and desire arising from a false understanding of the self comes right out of essential Buddhism. Like Buddhism, this document also promises that there is a cure for such difficulty. Saying no. 3 teaches that the follower, to grasp the meaning of the gospel, must cleanse the heart of its cravings. To understand the good news, one must begin with renunciation.

Renunciation, which the text equates with repentance, is not hatred of the world. The world is good (see no. 25). What is evil is that our egos, in their search for security in the world, have transformed simple needs into cravings. To prop up the ego, we humans desire much more than we need. We want things in order to make our very insecure egos secure and in so doing, of course, hurt both others and ourselves.

Renunciation, then, is disenchantment with the world. The world no longer enthralls. Renunciation is a return to simplicity, to what both Daoists and Buddhists have called our "Original Nature."[55] Renunciation is not a new law that Ye Su sets forth. Obedience to law is always the work of the ego. Renunciation is a work of the Spirit. Saying no. 41 explains what the Spirit is:

> **The Spirit is the kingdom made manifest. When the trees move their branches you know that the Spirit is there. The Spirit is your life. When you breathe, it is the Spirit that moves within you. When your breath flows perfectly with the Spirit, you are in the kingdom. Watch your breath.**

The last imperative "Watch your breath," indicates that this Religion of Light writer may have adopted some kind of meditational practice similar to that used by both Buddhists and Daoists. Saying no. 43 **"In all things be mindful."** also indicates strong Buddhist influence. A perusal of the *Sayings* reveals several other sections that also hint at the practice of meditation.

Ye Su's attitude toward the *psyche*, which in the West, would be translated as "soul," also seems very Buddhist. The *psyche*, like the five *skandhas* of Buddhism, is said in no. 44 to fall apart at death. Death for the *psyche* is taken to be inevitable because, as Ye Su says to Peter in no. 46, **"all component parts decay."** This is a direct quotation from several Buddhist sutras. In the *Mahaparinibbanasutta* these are among the last words the Buddha says.[56]

---

[55] A phrase often used by Zhuangzi.
[56] *Buddhist Suttas*, 114.

What is eternal in us is not the soul but the light, that illumination from the Source that makes us human. It is our craving that keeps us from resting in the light. We so identify with the perishable ego that our lives are spent trying futilely to prop it up and protect it. Thus we crave. There is nothing wrong with an ego *per se*. We have egos for good reason. What is wrong is that we do not comprehend the nature of the ego and thus try to defend the indefensible. Chan Buddhists, thoroughly aware of the ego's impermanence, might very well call the light our "Buddha nature." Like light, the Buddha nature makes seeing possible, but in itself blinds the eyes. It is always present, at the root of our being, but cannot be known. It can only be assumed.

It is clear, then, that the author is influenced by basic Buddhist ideas, but it is also evident that not all Buddhist sects made much impression upon him. For instance, although Pure Land's emphasis upon faith alone might appeal to some Christians, there are really no allusions to *Qing Tu* that I can see. The same may be said of Hua Yen and Tian-Tai Buddhism. The author has little interest in vast mythic scenarios and sweeping claims about Buddhahood. On the contrary, simplicity is the watchword. It would appear, then, that the author has much more affinity with Chan Buddhism. Although he employs no *kong ans* (those baffling stories designed by Chan Masters to shake the mind into *satori*), his emphasis is upon meditative emptiness and a message which is beyond words. My guess is that he would have much preferred the plainness of the Chan monastery to the highly elaborated vision of the Pure Land in the Mogao caves.

Daoist Concepts

Daoist influence, particularly from the *Dao De Jing*, is equally obvious throughout the work. Laozi, the supposed author of the Dao De Jing, emphasizes from the very beginning that Dao is beyond human comprehension. Hence, "The Dao that can be spoken of is not the eternal Dao."[57] Ye Su agrees, for he says in no. 5,

> **Do not think that I come to teach you about the Eternal Source. The Source is beyond all understanding. To speak about the Source is to create an idol.**

In many respects, the Source and the Dao are the same. Unknowable and incomprehensible, each is the source of all that is.

---

[57] *Dao De Jing*, no. 1.

Daoist influence is also strongly suggested in no. 39, for it is almost a paraphrase of section 42 of the *Dao De Jing*.

> **From the Source flows the One and the One contains the Two. The Two give birth to the Third, the Child of Adam, and from the Three flow forth all things.**

This saying is not only clearly influenced by Daoism but marks a radical shift in Christian theology. For the Biblical Jesus, the ultimate is "the Father in the heavens." He alone is God; there is no Mother God. In *The Secret Sayings* the Source is beyond comprehension and hence beyond all gender; yet from the Source bubbles up the One, the Primal Energy, and this Energy, which manifests itself as both active (yang) and passive (yin), contains two powers that we are later to learn in no. 61 are Father Heaven and Mother Earth. From them the Child of Humanity (Adam) is born. These three constitute the source of everything, In effect, the human is the ultimate unity of yin and yang, Mother and Father, and through this Child the universe is linked back to the Source.

Mention of a Divine Mother may, at first glance, seem to indicate a sort of polytheism, but such is clearly not the case. The Source is One, but it expresses itself (if I can use such an anthropomorphism) through duality. The Heavenly Father and the Mother have no reality apart from the one Source. The Two are the One and the One manifests as Two.

The formulation, Father, Mother, and Child looks vaguely like a new and very different version of the doctrine of the Trinity, but apparently it is not. No. 69 provides us with Ye Su's understanding of Trinitarian theology:

> **The Well, the Water, and the Drink of Eternity: the three are one.**

The Well is, of course, the Source, that hidden fountain beyond all words from which bubbles up all existence. The Water is that bubbling up, the kingdom itself, and the Drink is, one may suppose, the unity of the "drinker" and ultimate existence. The author here takes water, a very common Daoist metaphor for the Dao, and uses it to express Christian theology. Ye Su brings that drink of living water that, as John 4:14 says, bubbles up to eternal life.

Another passage of clearly Daoist inspiration is no. 36:

> **The true gifts of the Magi I give you: compassion, simplicity, and dare not be first in the world.**

These three gifts are taken directly from passage no. 67 of the *Dao De Jing* and represent a fusion of Daoist and Christian values.

Finally, one must note throughout the work the emphasis upon silence. Although no. 63 might be said to reflect the earliest ending of Mark's gospel, no. 64 provides an almost word-for-word quotation from the Dao De Jing, chapter 56.

Have you not heard that it was said of old, "Those who speak do not know; those who know do not speak."

Clearly, the author was thoroughly familiar with Laozi and refers to him often. What is somewhat strange, however, is that I have not been able to detect any particular references to later Daoist works like the *Wenzi*, the *Zhuangzi* or the *Liezi*. Others, however, may find references to these documents that I have missed.

One could make a case that there are discernible influences from The Scripture of Western Ascension (Xisheng Jing)[58] which was probably written in the fifth century, remained popular during the Tang dynasty, and could very well have been known our author. This work, like *The Secret Sayings*, is a rewriting of Scripture for a contemporary audience and incorporates in it much from the *Dao De Jing*. Therefore, it is difficult to know what in *The Sayings* was borrowed from Laozi and what might have been borrowed from this later work. Perhaps, I have missed possibilities, but I do not find many of the distinctive features of the *Xisheng*, however, in evidence in *The Secret Sayings*.

Whether our author made contact with the Celestial Masters or *shangqing* or *lingbao* sages is an open question. My guess is that he might have been repelled by the Celestial Master's organization and by the *lingbao's* public ceremonies. *Shangqing*, however, with its secret texts and master-disciple relationships would have been more to his liking. Perhaps his emphasis upon secrecy was derived from them. Basically, however, it was not sectarian Daoism but Laozi himself who was the influence. On almost every page one finds some hint that the author has devoted himself to the *Dao Do Jing*. My conclusion finally is that the author was moved, not by Daoist sectarianism but by a deep reading acquaintance with the old master.

---

[58] For a full introduction to this work, see Livia Kohn, *Taoist Mystical Philosophy, The Scripture of the Western Ascension*.

In any event, all these examples demonstrate beyond a shadow of a doubt that whoever wrote this work was under the strong influence of Buddhism and Daoism as well as, of course, Christianity. Even more than the *Jesus Sutras*, this work shows the radical transformation of Christianity in China as the author seeks to express his faith in a radically different and philosophically sophisticated environment. Paradoxically, *The Secret Sayings* also seems to be closer to the canonical gospels than the *Jesus Sutras*.

It should also be said in passing that although there seem to be few ideas derived from Confucianism, the format of the *Secret Sayings* with disciples asking the Master questions is very reminiscent of the *Lun Yu (The Analects)* of Confucius. Since the style is also somewhat like the *Gospel according to Thomas*, however, it is difficult to be sure that the structure of the work was due to Chinese influence.

Whether Confucianism influenced *The Secret Sayings* or not, Buddhist and Daoist influence appears obvious. At the same time, it must be observed that the text is not thoroughly "Chinafied." Peter Gregory and Patricia Buckley Ebrey have pointed out that all of the basic Chinese religious traditions share at least three basic emphases in common: 1) ancestor worship, 2) a bureaucratic view of the gods, and 3) an organismic view of the universe.[59] *The Secret Sayings* says nothing about ancestor worship and, given its view of life after death, would seem to deny its importance. Bureaucracy on either a human or divine level is, it would seem, an object of attack. Thus it is only the organismic view of the cosmos that is, in any way, adopted. In any event, now that Buddhist and Daoist influence is clear, let us turn more directly to how Christianity was transformed by these Chinese influences.

---

[59] Ebrey and Gregory, eds. *Religion and Society in T'ang and Sung,* 8-11.

The Theology of
The Secret Sayings of Ye Su

The Theology of *The Secret Sayings of Ye Su*

In many ways, this work is a masterpiece of Christian apologetics. That is, it employs already accepted Daoist and Buddhist ideas within a Confucian format in order to communicate the Gospel. In this respect, the author is no different from those many theologians in the West who restated Christianity in terms of Greek philosophy. Also like them the author produces through his or her efforts a unique form of Christianity. While Thomas Aquinas and the other scholastics developed a whole new vocabulary for theology, however, this author points to a whole new way of silence and an end to "God talk."

It also seems clear that the author is more than just an apologist. He or she also is using Chinese thought to attack some theological problems that have plagued Christianity for centuries. In other words, the author is selectively employing Chinese ideas to try to make better sense out of the gospels than earlier theologians had done.

One such problem, to which we have already alluded, is Biblical anthropomorphism. God in the Bible is regarded as the incomprehensible ultimate; yet He (and I use that term advisedly here) is also depicted as the heavenly Father, a King, a Judge, etc. In other words, the danger is always that the depiction of God in human terms runs the severe risk of idolatry. Can any deity depicted in anthropomorphic terms really be the Ultimate?

In the author's more Daoist metaphysics, the Source (Greek: *paygay*) is beyond all description. The image actually derives from John 4:14 in which Jesus speaks of a "spring (*paygay*) of water welling up to eternal life." This is the author's root image for his understanding of God and God's grace. But the author never mentions "God" or the "One Sacred Spirit" of the *Jesus Sutras*. For Ye Su the word Source or Spring is enough. There is simply an Unknowable Source that is the root of everything. From it bubbles up the One, that is the primal energy, which constantly emerges from the Unknown. The Source seems to be neither personal nor impersonal; yet it is at the root of our humanity.

The Primal Energy is seen as containing two complementary powers that are undoubtedly to be understood in terms of yin and yang, though these terms are never mentioned. Phenomenologically, they appear as Heaven and Earth. To use Western terminology, they are manifestations of transcendence and immanence. The author preserves the image of the Father in the heavens, but the Father alone is no longer the ultimate. Indeed, the Father can only be understood in reciprocal relation to the Mother. Heaven and Earth are relative terms that define each other. Father and Mother are equal. Only together do they point to the hidden source from which they flow and on which they depend. It should also be observed that while the Source is beyond understanding, beyond personality, the Father and the Mother provide an opportunity to relate personally to the ultimate.

In formulating his vision in this way, he solves another problem in Christian theology, that is, the lack of a maternal, feminine power. Roman Catholicism has attempted to meet this need by enthroning Mary as the Mother of God, but there has always seemed something askew about this, for the Father and Mother in this formulation are by no means equal. The Father is infinite while Mary, important as she may be, is still a human raised up to the level of near divinity. The roots of gender inequality are clearly in evidence. It is interesting that a representative of the Church of the East, which did not accept the cult of Mary as the Mother of God, should introduce the maternal power in this way.

For *The Secret Sayings,* the Source is beyond all gender, while the Father and the Mother are equals. This is, then, reflected in the author's depiction of the female followers, particularly Mary Magdalene, as being quite on a par with the other disciples. In fact, Mary is identified as the beloved disciple, the one disciple who understands best what Ye Su is about.

Another problem that the author seeks to solve is the role of the Church in the spiritual life, and does so in a most radical way. Clearly, the author has experienced deep problems within the Christian community and reacts strongly to what he believes is the Church's corruption and blindness. Therefore he writes in no. 49:

> **Judas said, "let us organize ourselves with a president and officers so that our movement may be more effective." Ye Su said, "Agape does not hold to order. The more you organize, the more your organization will become but one more institution of craving. Soon you will have some men ruling over others. Some will be forced to bow to their masters. There will be ordinances and laws and taboos. People will begin to think that faith is just subscribing to a set of ideas and the kingdom will become a fossil to be put upon the shelf along with all the other archaic doctrines. Then there will be persecutions and wars carried out in my name as the blind lead the blind into disaster. No, Judas, call no person Father or Rabbi or the Reverend or your Holiness. All of this comes from the craving of this**

world and will only end in violence and disorder. The kingdom comes as a miracle and miracles cannot be contained.

It may be said that much of this position can be traced back to the Jesus of the canonical gospels, for Jesus repeatedly attacks the religious authorities as hypocrites and tells his disciples not to use titles like Father and Rabbi. (Matthew 23:1-12). In this passage, *The Secret Sayings* elaborates upon this theme, emphasizing how dangerous Church organization can be. The great transformation in which craving is overcome and the simplicity of human nature is recovered is the result of a spiritual miracle. Organizations, however, cannot depend upon the continuation of miracles and so devise other means for survival. The result is that the organization quickly becomes a new and very dangerous example of human craving and egotism. Ye Su seems to have foreseen the whole bloody history of the Christian Church, for he predicts all those persecutions and holy wars carried on in his name that are so opposed to the kingdom.

In no. 52 Ye Su particularly warns against imperial and national churches, for they are bound to be impediments to the kingdom, while in no. 53 the Holy Church is depicted as a great beast which devours everything in its path. Therefore he says in no.54,

> **Keep my teaching secret; cast no pearls before swine, lest the great beast overhear the words and destroy.**

The message of *The Secret Sayings*, then, is profoundly opposed to an organized, hierarchical church, for that is bound to distort his words and destroy the kingdom. In this sense, the author could be said to be the originator of the "No Church" movement. From the point of view of most Christians, nothing could be clearer or more "heretical" than this message: Avoid the Church. Do not turn the kingdom into an organization. When you meet, just meet as friends (no.50), but do not emphasize the organization. The kingdom has nothing to do with ecclesiastical hierarchy. One can see why a Catholic priest refused to translate this for publication.

Not only does the author raise great question marks about the structure of the Church. It would also, on the basis of what is said, be difficult to construct a liturgy or join in ordinary corporate worship. When the disciples ask Ye Su to teach them to pray he does not offer any version of the Lord's Prayer. Reflecting what Jesus says in the Sermon on the Mount (Matt. 6:5-6) Ye Su in no.17 is quoted as saying,

Go into your inner room and close the door. Do not pray in public as the addicts do, for that is idolatry. Do not try to tell the Eternal Source what to do, for that is presumptuous. Just listen. Listen, I say, listen. Those who have ears, let them hear.

If this admonition (like Matt. 6:5-6) were to be taken seriously, one might wonder how public worship could ever become a reality. Certainly most Christian liturgies would not be acceptable because they all contain public prayer. Nevertheless, in nos. 29 and 30 Ye Su accepts the rite of baptism while in nos. 59, 60, and 61 Ye Su does seem to institute what has been called the Last Supper or the Eucharist. There are no blessings or prayers, just the breaking of bread and drinking of wine, so the commandment not to pray in public is preserved, but the basis for a ritual is there. Perhaps worship for the author would be something like that of the Quakers in which one waits in silence upon the Source, though it might also include music (no. 40) and dance (no. 65) as well as the breaking of bread and drinking of wine. In any event, it would be quite different from the usual liturgies of Christendom.

Just as Ye Su attacks both Church organization and public prayer, so he also undercuts another prominent feature of Western Christianity, that is, doctrine itself. no. 63 reads as follows:

> **Ye Su asked Mary, "What shall you do when I return from the dead?' Mary said, "If you were to return from the dead, I would observe awe-struck silence and speak to no one about it." Ye Su said, "You have learned well, Mary. You shall be my apostle.**

Then the author inserts the typically Daoist saying in no. 64, "**Those who speak do not know, those who know do not speak.**" When, in no. 65 Peter presses him on this, arguing that you can't proclaim the good news without saying *something*. Ye Su smiles and simply leads his disciples in "The Circular Dance of Joy." Clearly, the message is that the kingdom is to be danced; it cannot be articulated in words.

Thus this work points in exactly the opposite direction from most Western versions of Christianity that have devoted themselves to doctrines, theologies, confessions, and creeds. Much blood has been spilled over which verbal formulation is best. The Roman Catholic and Orthodox Churches parted company over a single letter in the Nicene Creed. This author is radically anti-creedal because, for him, the essence of the faith is beyond words. The Source is beyond words, the

Water and Light of Life are beyond words; existence is beyond words. Ye Su offers us, not new ideas, but a drink from the Waters of Eternity that flow forth from the Source. If words are devised to define what is meant by this, soon all that will be left are words. And then people will persecute others about them.

Ye Su's own words are but pointers to an unspeakable inner transformation that is begun with renunciation and is nurtured by meditation, a transformation that leads to the death of the old self and to rebirth in the Spirit. The author, reflecting upon the death of Ye Su reveals the secret:

> And you must die. Your craving, born of your prideful ego, must perish. Your death, like that of Ye Su, will be dreadfully painful, for the addiction is so intense and has gone on so long. Earth will tremble and Heaven will grow dark before the veil is rent, the Holy of Holies revealed, and the light, the eternal light, begins to shine. (no. 68)

The point of following Ye Su is not to believe in doctrines or join an organization but to undergo the dramatic inner transformation that leads to the kingdom. In other words, to use the famous imperative from John's Gospel, "You must be born anew."

In significant respects, this vision of Ye Su, which so emphasizes light, is reminiscent of the religion of Mani that swept through much of central Asia and then Europe with its own religion of light. Mani (?216-?276), however, was a dualist, setting the Light over against Darkness, the Good against the Bad, the Spirit against the Flesh. For Mani, the body, matter, darkness are the enemy. Therefore, the inner core of Mani's followers were highly ascetic.

Although Ye Su knows the reality of human corruption, he is not a dualist at all. For him the body and sexuality are gifts from the Mother (nos. 14, 15, 25, 27). Therefore there is no hint of asceticism or a call to celibacy here. While Mani counsels people to forsake the flesh, Ye Su teaches his disciples how to play with children and how to dance. He teaches that music, poetry, and art all flow out of that Eternal Source called the "Paygay." He calls people to open their eyes to the light that plays all around them and to love that light in each other. Without organization or dogma, this is a teaching of the sharing of light, love, and peace.

Ye Su is realistic. He recognizes the grip that egoistic craving has upon people and how it corrupts both individuals and societies. As devastating as this grip is, however, it is not the final answer, for the power of the kingdom can loosen it. The light can shine through; beyond death there is life.

What makes this theology different from most classical theologies is that salvation is not something done *to* the individual, but is rather the fruit of a power that is eternally within. The light has always been and always will be. Ye Su is not conceived as an historical character who dies to pay a divine debt and hence to take away human sin through forgiveness, but rather simply a person who awakens followers to the water of eternity and to the divine light. The kingdom is not a new reality; it has always been "at hand." Emphasis upon the holy history (*Heilsgeschichte,* as German theologians have called) is missing. Ye Su is significant because he is, to use the words of Paul Tillich, "transparent to the Ground of Being."

Whether his basically anti-ecclesiastical, anti-liturgical, anti-doctrinal stance could have ever been accepted by his fellow Christians is an interesting question. Certainly the author knew that in some parts of Christendom many of his ideas would have been met with fierce resistance. Even in the somewhat freer Church of the East it is clear there would have been some severe criticism. After all, he was attacking what many believed to be the essence of the faith. Therefore, he names these *The Secret Sayings* and warns against sharing them openly. The collection of sayings ends with these words,

Hide my secrets until the time is fulfilled. Beware the beast.

Having looked briefly at the major theological (or anti-theological) thrust of this work, let us now turn more specifically to each of the sayings.

Notes and Comments

The Secret Sayings of Ye Su
Notes and Comments

1. To the multitude I speak only in parables, for the world is drunk with its own importance, addicted to its own pride. Drunken understanding is worse than drunken ignorance.

    See Mark 4:10-12, Gospel of Thomas, 28.
    I take συνηθης in a strong sense to mean "addicted" rather than simply "habituated to the customary," though, in fact, much addiction is simple habituation to what everyone accepts.

    Ye Su begins by explaining why his teachings are, in a sense, secret. The world is gripped by an addiction that arises out of the human ego. When someone who is so addicted tries to grasp his inner teachings, the teachings are bound to become corrupted. Hence the title, *The Secret Sayings of Ye Su*. In truth, spiritual preparation is needed before the sayings can be properly understood.

2. To you I will explain everything, if you will but sober up.

    Buddhists often describe ignorance, which is the cause of human suffering, as like intoxication.

    To receive these inner teachings, the disciples themselves must sober up and rid themselves of their craving. They must, in the words of Soren Kierkegaard, make motions of "infinite resignation." Kierkegaard writes:

    > The infinite resignation is the last stage prior to faith, so that one who has made this movement has not faith; for only in the infinite resignation do I become clear to myself with respect to my eternal validity, and only then can there be any question of grasping existence by virtue of faith.[60]

---

[60] Soren Kierkegaard, *Fear and Trembling and The Sickness Unto Death*, 57.

3.   Peter said, "How, Master, can I sober up? Show me the way. Ye Su said, "To be my disciple you must renounce everything. Cleanse your heart of the world and its cravings."

> The verb, *apotasso* (**αποτασσω**), here translated renounce, means "to say goodbye to or forsake" hence "to renounce." Craving translates the word **επιθυμια**.
>
> Compare with the First Liturgical Sutra. "So Simon, if anyone wants to follow the Way of Triumph they (*sic*) must clear their minds, and set aside all wanting and doing." [61]

Ye Su teaches that the way to the kingdom is renunciation. It is to give up the craving of the world. Nonetheless, his message is neither ascetic nor world denying. (See Nos, 14, 27, 55). Perhaps, some lines from the Bhagavadgita will help us in understanding Ye Su.

> When he gives up desires in his mind,
> is content with the self within himself,
> then he is said to be a man
> whose insight is sure, Arjuna.
>
> When suffering does not disturb his mind,
> when his craving for pleasures has vanished.
> when attraction, fear, and anger are gone,
> he is called a sage whose thought is sure.[62]

In a word, the renunciator is in the world but not of it. One acts, but without the craving for fame or fortune or even some formulation of the truth.

M.K. Gandhi, in his famous commentary on the Bhagavad Gita, emphasizes the importance of acting without attachment, even to what is normally thought of as good. He writes, "To love God means to be free from attachment to any work. We should of course do work, but without egotistic attachment to it, simply for the love of God."[63]

---

[61] Palmer, *op. cit.,* 190. See also 226.

[62] Barbara Stoller Miller, trans. *The Bhagavad-gita,* 37.

[63] M.K. Gandhi, *The Bhagavadgita,* 229.

4. Peter said, "Teacher, if I renounce everything, how can I live?" Ye Su said, "What I ask is not a law, for no law can demand the impossible. Only the Spirit can achieve the impossible. The world tells us that complete renunciation is impossible, but consider the birds of the air. They have no regular employment or storage barns; yet they live more happily than we. Renunciation is a work of the Spirit that never ends; it is freedom from the craving of the world. It is a life of genuine simplicity. It is the disenchantment of the world. Renunciation is repentance. It is to turn and go in exactly the opposite direction."

> Renunciation, then, is not a new law laid upon people, but is the fruit of the Spirit. It is not fleeing from the world but the renunciation of craving for the world. Renunciation is neither anorexia nor impotence. Natural desires are healthy and good. In order to "prop up" what appears to be a very frail ego, the psyche corrupts all natural desires by turning them into cravings. The psyche becomes enchanted, always looking for ways to justify and prop itself up. The result invariably is greed and hatred and the concomitant suffering.

> Renunciation, which is here equated with repentance (*metanoia*)), is to see through the enchantments of the world. It is to come to yourself. Or rather, it is to see through the illusion of the self. For Buddhism it is the self, conceived as a substantial reality, that is the major cause of human disaster. To "see into one's own nature" is to see through the ephemeral ego.

5. Do not think that I come to teach you about the Eternal Source. The Source is beyond all understanding. To speak about the Source is to create an idol. I come to proclaim the kingdom. Nevertheless, to live in the kingdom is to be one with the Source.

> *Paygay (Πηγη)*—: source, root, well, spring.
> See John 4:14 "The water that I shall give him will become in him a spring (πηγη) of water welling up to eternal life."

> Throughout this text, the author refers to πηγη (the Source or Spring) rather than to God. The Source is hidden; yet everything flows from it.

The kingdom is found by drinking from this incomprehensible Source of Being. Any Daoist would find it easy to understand the Source as *Dao*, for the *Dao De Jing* regularly uses water as a metaphor for the *Dao* (See *Dao De Jing*, nos. 13 and 78). See also *The Secret Sayings* no. 69 for a Trinitarian understanding of this metaphor.

6. **James said, "May I help you to rule the kingdom?" Ye Su said, "If you wish to rule, you are far from the kingdom and from me."**

    See Matthew 20:21.

    James asks the old question, assuming that the kingdom is a realm to be ruled. Ye Su makes clear that James has radically misunderstood. It is the Source's kingdom, where the Source rules.
    Basileus *(Βασιλεως)*, the word rendered kingdom, could also be translated as "reign." In either case, it refers to an hereditary, benign rule and not a tyranny. I have preferred to keep to the more traditional translation, but it is clear that the kingdom is the locus where the Source's power rules, It may be significant that the other *Jesus Sutras* do not emphasize the kingdom at all.

7. **The kingdom is like seeds sown upon the earth; if the soil is good, the seeds will sprout and grow.**

    See Mark 4:3-9, 26-29, 30-32.

    Compare with *The Scripture of the Western Ascension 5.2* "(The image of Tao) can be compared to the seed of a tree. Before it sprouts one cannot see branches, leaves, and fruits."[64]

    At the beginning of this work, the images used are of the earth: the spring of water, the seeds in the earth, etc. Then, in the last part of the text, the heavenly symbol of light becomes more frequent. It takes both water and light to make the seeds of the kingdom grow.

---

[64] Kohn, *op. cit.*, 237.

8. **The seed of the kingdom is within you. Nourish it.**

> See Luke 17:21
>
> The preposition ϵντοϛ usually is translated "within" although it may be trans-lated "among." Given the other sayings, "within" seems more appropriate.
>
> What Ye Su speaks of is natural to us, but we have become blinded to it by our craving. (Compare with the Great Stele: "Originally they had no desire, but under the influence of Satan, they abandoned their pure and simple goodness for the glitter and the gold."[65]) When renunciation becomes a reality, the kingdom begins to grow. Renouncing germinates the seed. Meditation nourishes it.

9. **Philip asked, "When will the kingdom come?" Ye Su said, "When the time is full the seed sprouts up and grows you know not how, but you will know when the harvest is ready. Only be sure that you water with care."**

> Philip assumes that the kingdom is some sort of historical reality that will come in time. Ye Su signals that the kingdom grows in each one of us if we nourish it. Ye Su, in this work, seems to have little interest in his-torical eschatology. This fact maybe important for interpreting saying no. 72.

10. **Peter said, "Show us a sign that we may believe." Ye Su said, "The kingdom is its own sign. Do you not know that the deaf hear, the lame dance, and the blind receive their sight? Have you no eyes to see?"**

> See Matthew 15: 31; Luke 7:22.
>
> The only miracles that this gospel knows are the miracles of the Spirit. Ye Su here speaks of the spiritual deafness, lameness, and blindness which craving brings. When the great disenchantment takes place, people begin to hear and see and dance again. Those are the signs of the kingdom. The kingdom is the restoration of one's original nature.

---

[65] Palmer, *op. cit.*, 225

11. **Mary said, "I love you, Ye Su." Ye Su said, "That is a good start; the kingdom is born from love."**

> The word translated "love" is agapao and therefore has nothing to do with erotic attraction. The kingdom is born out of self-giving, over-flowing love. It is noteworthy that it is Mary, of all the disciples, who makes the break-through and understands. *Agape* is a sign, perhaps *the* sign, of the kingdom.

> Some interpreters have made much of a possible love affair between Jesus and Mary Magdalene. Here there is a love affair, but it is entirely spiritual in nature.

12. **Recognize the kingdom where it is. It is in the eyes of every person you meet. If you see the kingdom in me, you will see it everywhere. If you know the kingdom in any face, you will know me.**

> Compare with The Third Liturgical Sutra I.6.[66]

> The kingdom is not some foreign realm imposed upon us but is the most natural realm imaginable. It is there, shining in every eye. Once you have met the kingdom, it becomes visible everywhere. In this sense the kingdom is among us, for it is through interaction that the kingdom becomes known. What is unnatural is not to know the kingdom.

> The Sufi poet, Jelaluddin Rumi, writes,

> > The light you give off
> > did not come from the pelvis.
> > Your features did not begin in semen.
> > Don't try to hide inside anger
> > radiance that cannot be hidden.[67]

---

[66] Palmer,*op. cit.,* 189.
[67] Jelaluddin Rumi, *The Essential Rumi*, 74.

13. One day, as Ye Su taught his disciples, Peter left to quiet children who were playing in the courtyard and disturbing his concentration. Ye Su asked, "Where are you going?" Peter replied, "To make the children be quiet." Ye Su said, "Do not do that; let us go outside." The children were playing a game, laughing and showing great delight. Ye Su said, "Behold, the kingdom is like this, full of joy and gladness; let us join them." And so Ye Su and his disciples played with the children all afternoon.

See Matthew 19:14

Jesus was quite unique among the teachers of antiquity because of his very positive attitude toward children. "Of such," he said, "are the kingdom of heaven." In no. 13 Ye Su not only commends children but actually joins in their games. The tradition of holy men playing games with children is a fairly common one in China and Japan. Wuzi, a fat monk often pictured with five (*wu*) children climbing on him, is said to answer the prayers of the childless. The figure of Budai Heshang, an immensely fat monk with a canvass bag who also frequently is depicted as covered with little children, must antedate the ninth century, for at that time Budai was included among the Sixteen Arhats. In Japan, Budai becomes Hotei who is listed among the Seven Deities of Happiness. This tradition was carried on historically by Ryokan, an eighteenth century Japanese monk-poet who loved to play the game of *temari* with the children who always seemed to swarm about him.

> In my sleeve the colored ball worth a thousand in gold.
> I dare say no one's as good at *temari* as me!
> And if you ask what it's all about—
> one—two—three—four—five—six—seven[68]

If the author of the *Secret Sayings* was repeating a common tradition about Jesus, one must at least entertain the possibility that it was from the Religion of Light that the Buddhist traditions of Wuzi and Budai developed. Surely, there is little emphasis upon children in either Indian Buddhism or classical Daoism.

---

[68] *Ryokan: Zen Monk-Poet of Japan*, 72.

14. Peter said, "Let us fast and punish our bodies so that the kingdom will come." Ye Su said, "Your body is the gift of our Mother. Treat your body with holiness and respect. It is not your body that causes your addiction; it is your psyche. Clean the inside of the cup; that is what matters."

See Matthew 23:25-26.

This is a passage that distinguishes Ye Su from Mani and many other ascetic teachers. Ye Su not only teaches that we should treat our bodies with holiness and respect, he calls the body a gift from the Mother. For Ye Su, the body and matter are not the source of evil. How could they be, for they flow out of the Source? It is the ego that, though not evil, has become corrupted through addiction. Spiritual problems do not result from bodily needs; they result from our psychological addictions.

Respect for the body and the Mother who gives it has important ecological implications. Nature is not the enemy to be repressed and overcome, as Genesis 1:28 would seem to imply, but something (perhaps even someone) to be respected and treated with reverence.[69] Human craving is what destroys the earth; it is respect for the Mother, who flows out of the Source that can save it.

Ye Su's attitude is far closer to classical Daoism that has regularly emphasized our oneness with nature than it is to classical Christianity that has often emphasized that the body and matter are enemies to be overcome. Ye Su also presents a very different attitude from that of Sir Francis Bacon, the great scientific hero, who said that we should torture Nature so that she will reveal her secrets.

15. **Your body is the temple of the Holy Spirit. What other temple do you need?**

See 1 Corinthians 6:19.

This is the first hint of the author's very anti-ecclesiastical stance. If the Holy Spirit dwells within you, if you can find a way to the Source here, in the body, why do you need the Temple, its priesthood, and all those

---

[69] Compare Genesis 1:28 in which humans are called to "subdue" the earth.

rules and regulations? The point is to find the kingdom within. It is noteworthy that in no. 68 all those apparently external events connected with the crucifixion (the earthquake, the darkening of the sky, and the rending of the temple veil) are all internalized, as descriptions of the radical transformation.

One is reminded of the trenchant words of the Indian poet Kabir (16th C.):

> What use is reading
> The Vedas and Puranas?
> You only become burdened
> Like a donkey.
> You never learned the reality
> Of Ram's name—
> How will you get across?[70]

Like Ye Su, Kabir taught that all that really matters is knowing that inner, indescribable power that the poet named Ram.

16. **Close the windows, shut the doors, keep the foolishness and violence of the world away. When your mind is free of foolishness and empties into the great Sea, then you will be close.**

See *Dao De Jing* no. 56.

This is the first major hint of meditational practice and the influence seems clearly Daoist. It is not enough just to renounce. One must, at times, close out the outside world in order to free the psyche of its foolishness. There is no explanation of what it means for the mind to empty into the Great Sea, but it is surely the language of a mystic. We are reminded of Edwin Arnold's famous phrase,

> Om Mani Padme Hum, the Sunrise Comes!
> The dewdrop slips into the shining sea![71]

---

[70] Kabir, *Songs of Kabir from the Adi Granth,* 209.
[71] Edwin Arnold, *The Light of Asia or The Great Renunciation,* 238.

As in *The Secret Sayings*, light and water are joined as symbols of enlightenment by Arnold. Buddhists would doubtless call this slipping into the sea *samhadi*.

Hui Neng, who may very well have been a contemporary of the author wrote: "It is like the great sea which fathers all the flowing streams, and merges together the small waters and the large waters into one. This is seeing into your own nature."[72]

17. The disciples said, "Teach us to pray." Ye Su replied, "Go into your inner room and close the door. Do not pray in public as the addicts do, for that is idolatry. Do not try to tell the Eternal Source what to do, for that is presumptuous. Just listen. Listen, I say, listen. Those who have ears, let them hear."

See Matthew 6:5-6

When the disciples ask for instruction about prayer, we might reasonably expect from *The Secret Sayings* some version of the Lord's Prayer, but Ye Su urges his disciples to get beyond words in order to listen to the Word from the Source. Again we are given a hint of the meditational practice that the author taught. Like the Quakers he teaches his disciples to "wait upon the Spirit."

18. Peter asked, "How should we live? Teach us the Law." Ye Su said, "The Law only cleans the outside of the cup but leaves the inside full of foul debris. If you think I have come with a new Law, you are wrong. The Law was given for hardness of heart. The wine of the kingdom dissolves the hardness."

See Luke 11:39 and Matthew 23:25-26.

Ye Su is not opposed to laws for society, but he sees that the law can only restrain people; it cannot restore them to their own original nature that has become distorted through craving. His mention of wine may be reminiscent of the second chapter of John in which Jesus transforms the water of Jewish law into the wine of the spirit.

---

[72] Hui Neng, *op. cit.*, 150.

19. The world's addiction to the ego creates hearts of stone.

> "Hearts of stone" and "hardness of heart" are common Biblical images.
>
> Ye Su sees that our addictions cannot be prevented through law, because they are all based upon a false view of the self. If one addiction is curtailed by law, then, another will take its place. Thus none of the wars on drugs and other forms of addiction ever succeed. Until the kingdom becomes a reality, one addiction will follow another.

20. The world needs laws, for craving creates conflict, but when the kingdom comes, there is only the law of love. "Love your neighbor as yourself:" there is nothing more that is needed. To love your neighbor is to love the Eternal Source.

> Ye Su is not a social antinomian. In this world, laws and punishments are a necessity, but when the kingdom comes, all the individual needs is the law of love. In fact, the law of love is not really a law at all, but a profound impulse of compassion that emerges when the old enchantments are destroyed and the kingdom begins to grow within. Love is the kingdom made manifest.

21. Everything I say is of the kingdom, not of the Law. Sing and dance for the good news.

> Ye Su offers genuinely good news about which one should celebrate. Rediscovering the precious treasure buried in the heart is a matter of great rejoicing.
>
> Renunciation may sound gloomy, but leads to exactly the opposite result. One may guess that the famous Tang poet Li Po (pin yin: Li Bo) also knew something of the wine of good news:
>
> 9/9, Out Drinking on Dragon Mountain
>
> 9/9, out drinking on Dragon Mountain,
> I'm an exile among yellow blossoms smiling.

> Soon drunk, I watch my cap tumble in wind,
> Dance in love—a guest the moon invites.[73]

It may be, of course, that the poet speaks only of a drinking spree, but he was, in fact, a Daoist priest who, undoubtedly, used the metaphor of drinking wine to speak of deeper and more cosmic joy. Hence, I include his poetry here. Metaphorical parallels are to be found in much Sufi poetry.

22. **There once was a pearl merchant who sought the world's most perfect pearl. He traveled the earth, enduring great perils and sufferings, but returned to his home tired, impoverished, and empty-handed. Then his wife discovered the pearl he sought for so long in the headband he had worn on the journey.**

    See Matthew 13:45-46.

    This saying represents a very old category of stories that is found in both east and west. One is reminded of the 8th chapter of the Lotus Sutra in which a beggar discovers, after years of hardship, that he has had a precious jewel sewn in his garment all along. What he spent his life looking for, he discovers he already possessed. It may significant that here it is the wife, the feminine side of the person, who discovers the pearl. The yang seeks without what the yin finds within. So it is with the kingdom. Ye Su comes to wake us up to what is already ours, if we would but recognize it.

23. **John said, "Teach us about the kingdom." Ye Su said, "Do not look for the kingdom as though it will appear in one place or another. The kingdom is here, now. Nevertheless, you must prepare for its wonderful appearance. It is like a flash of lightning that illumines all. So do not close your eyes, even for a moment. The kingdom is like the leading lady of the drama who waits in the wings for her cue. She is there, but you do not see her."**

    See: Luke 17:20
    The vocabulary in the penultimate line is that of the Greek theater.

---

[73] Li Po, *The Selected Poems of Li Po*, 97.

The nature of the kingdom is paradoxical. It is here, right now; yet it also waits unseen in the wings. One must simply trust that in due time the kingdom will appear if we will but nourish it. The kingdom as a sudden flash of lightning is comparable to Chan Buddhism's view of *satori,* of sudden enlightenment.

24. **The world is addicted, always craving, never satisfied. Because the world craves, there is suffering and violence and hate. Those who succeed in the world are the unhappiest of all.**

Ye Su turns the values of the world upside down. Success in the world is success in craving, in propping up the ego and this is exactly what prevents the coming of the kingdom. (See also no. 35.) Thus success in the world and the failure to find the kingdom are virtually synonymous. Nevertheless, the kingdom is available to anyone who will but turn around.

Bo Zhu-I, the famous Tang poet, describes the world in a similar way:

> Don't go climbing up to the blue clouds—
> The blue clouds are rife with passion and hate,
> Everyone a wise man, bragging of know-how and vision,
> Flattening each other in the scramble for merit and power.
> Fish get chowdered because they swallow the bait,
> Moths burn up when they bumble into a lamp.
> Better come drink wine with me,
> let yourself go, get roaring, roaring drunk.[74]

For Ye Su, one should become drunk with the wine of the kingdom, for it is that wine that melts and transforms the heart's hardness. See also nos. 18 and 61.

25. **Do not despise the world or its people; the seeds of the kingdom are everywhere. Delight in everything.**

Despite the world's craving which leads inevitably to violence and suffering, Ye Su counsels a positive attitude toward the world, for the seeds of

---

[74] Po Chu-I, *Selected Poems,* 130.

the kingdom are everywhere. This world constantly flows forth from the Source. Although corrupted by ego-craving, the world is not evil.

26. Peter said, "Some effeminate men wanted to see you, but I sent them away." Ye Su said, "You were wrong to do that, Peter. Did I not tell you that the seeds of the kingdom are everywhere?" "But supposing they will not reform their ways?" "Think not of the faults of others, Peter, for no one has achieved true righteousness. Have more faith in the power of the kingdom. Therefore I say, do not judge others or censure them. Look only to your own craving."

Effeminate men: μαλακοί. See I Corinthians 6: 9 where Paul uses the same word.
See Matthew 7:1-5

Apparently, there are no really new problems, for the whole question of homosexuality that is now so bothering churches is raised here. Interestingly, Ye Su does not condemn the effeminate men, but welcomes them, finding in them, as in everyone else, the seeds of the kingdom. What he does criticize is judging and censuring others. The essential problem of humans is not sexual orientation but craving. Judging others is a way of justifying oneself and hence is an expression of ego-craving.

27. Nathaniel asked, "Must we become celibate for the sake of the kingdom?" Ye Su said, "No, sexual desire is a gift from our Mother and we must give thanks for her gifts and use them wisely. Celibacy does not end the craving but only intensifies it. True marriage is the reunification of Adam, and is the great and holy Mystery. Only the Child of Adam enters the kingdom."

Sexual desire: eros (ερος)

"Child of Adam" could be translated "Child of Humanity." It is equivalent to the Biblical "Son of Man." That is to say, although the text does use the Biblical name, Adam, it seems to refer, not to some primal ancestor from the distant past but rather to humanity as a whole. It should also be noted that in Genesis "Adam" is male and female together. When Adam is split in two the two halves are *ish* (male) and *ishshah* (female). It is only after the eating of the fruit of the knowledge of good and evil that the male assumes the name Adam and calls ishshah Chawah or, in Greek, Eve.

Again Ye Su, unlike many religious teachers, is very positive about sexuality and marriage that he calls "the great and holy Mystery." One should renounce ego-craving, not true marriage. Indeed, it could be argued that true marriage can only take place with renunciation. True marriage reflects the union of heaven and earth. It is through that union that the Child of Humanity is born and it is through that child that we can return to the Source.

Some might argue that this passage may reflect the influence of the Celestial Masters who employed ritualized sexual intercourse in order to participate symbolically in the creation process through which Heaven and Earth, yin and yang are reunited.[75] By the Tang dynasty, ritual sex was probably no longer practiced very much among the Celestial Masters, but the theory remained.[76] One might also hypthesize that there was influence from the Tantric tradition of India, for the Tantras also place positive emphasis upon the body. The Shiva-Shakti relationship is, in some ways, parallel to that of the Father-Mother of this work. It is probably more likely, however, that the view of marriage expressed here is derived from the Hebrew Scriptures and such books as the Song of Songs.

28. **I am the light that shines in the darkness, the light that enlightens every person. You have always known me, though today, in your blindness, you do not recognize me.**

See John 1:1-13.

Now the author introduces the metaphor of light. Just as the universe is both Father Heaven and Mother Earth, so the kingdom is both the water flowing from the earthly Source and the heavenly light emanating from the heavenly Source.

Together Heaven and Earth unite to create the Child of Humanity. Ye Su is that Child and when we cleanse our hearts through renunciation we discover that we and the Child are also one.

---

[75] Kristofer Schipper, " Taoism: the Story of the Way." in Stephen Little with Shawn Eichman, *Taoism and the Arts of China*, 42.

[76] For an interesting collection of texts about Daoist sexual practice, see Douglas Wile, *Art of the Bedchamber*.

29. Only the naked should baptize the naked.

See the Gospel of Thomas no. 37.

Nakedness is a symbol of renunciation and the wisdom gained thereby. The renunciant puts away all those ego-cravings to stand without means of visible modesty or defense, relying solely upon the emptiness of No Thingness to guide. Only someone who has achieved this state should take it upon his or herself to initiate others. Thus, like many Eastern traditions, this text emphasizes the importance of the Guru, the teacher who has received not only external legitimization but internal transformation. It is interesting that the author does assume the reality of some rite of baptism, a rite that remains unmentioned in the Jesus Sutras.

30. Running floodwaters of the earth and the unpredictable winds of heaven; a plunge of death into the waters, the fluttering of the dove: the Child of Adam is born.

See Matthew 3:16-17.

This was perhaps the most difficult of the sayings to translate properly, for the grammar is most peculiar. The text seems to reflect the story of Jesus' baptism as a prototype for all Christian baptism. In true baptism, one is born from Heaven and Earth as the Child of Adam. One becomes Ye Su. Thus baptism is not just an external ritual but involves inner spiritual transformation. It is interesting how nature and grace here become one. The image of wind upon the water is reminiscent of Genesis 1:2 that describes when light was first brought forth. Creation and re-creation are the same. For this author, as for many Daoists, there is no real distinction between spirit and matter, The Source and the universe, religion and natural science.

31. Peter said, "Why do you allow women to follow you? Should not only men be disciples?" Ye Su said, "Peter, Peter, are you so blind? Do you not see that the seeds of the kingdom are planted in both women and men and that in the kingdom there is no difference between them? We are all the union of male and female and therefore are in ourselves both male and female. Until you realize that, the kingdom will be far away. To remind you of your blindness, when I appear in glory, Mary shall see me first. She is my beloved disciple."

Compare The Gospel of Thomas, No. 114.

Peter, as usual, represents the conventional attitude of religious groups, this time toward women. There are, needless to say, Peters to be found not only in Christianity but also in Judaism, Buddhism, Daoism, and certainly Confucianism. Muslims, following the Quran (4:34) have often been quite blatant in declaring women inferior. Ye Su, however, attacks such attitudes as blindness. Not only does he declare male and female equal; he calls Mary his beloved disciple and thus would seem to identify her as the author of the Gospel of John. In this egalitarian attitude he agrees wholeheartedly with the Religion of Light. It is interesting that the author, unlike many thinkers of that time period from both East and West, knew that biologically each person is a union of male and female rather than essentially the male sperm simply nurtured by the mother.

Although Buddhism often expresses rather misogynistic tendencies, there are also other more positive passages about women. One thinks, for instance, of the twelfth chapter of the Lotus Sutra[77] and the seventh chapter of the Vimalakirtinirdesa sutra.[78] Daoism also sometimes emphasized the importance of the feminine. For instance, Laozi speaks of *Dao* as the Mother. Thus, although Chinese civilization was decidedly patriarchal, the attitude toward women taken in this text might well have found a sympathetic hearing among some Buddhists and Daoists.

32. The kingdom is *agape* made manifest among us. It is the one great miracle. If you know *agape*, the kingdom comes.

I have retained the Greek *agape* (αγαπη) because the word "love" has a variety of connotations in English and may, in fact, denote egotistical craving. Perhaps "compassion" could have been used, but that word has overtones of pity. *Agape,* in any event, is that overwhelming sense of common humanity and oneness that bubbles up like a miracle from the Source.

---

[77] *The Lotus Sutra,* trans. Burton Watson, 186-87.
[78] *The Holy Teaching of Vimalakirti,* translated by Robert A. F. Thurman, 56-63.

33. *Agape* is not just a feeling in the human heart but grows among us. Act in *agape*; then there will be feeling.

> *Agape* is not just sentimental tingles. It is a bond that transcends individuals and binds them together. It is the bond that binds the Lover and the Beloved. Rumi says,
>
>> Borrow the beloved's eyes.
>> Look through them and you'll see the beloved's face
>> Everywhere. No tiredness, no jaded boredom.
>> "I shall be your eye and your hand and your loving."
>> Let that happen, and things
>> you have hated will become helpers.[79]

34. Judas asked, "What should we do for the poor?" Ye Su answered, "Love the poor, but do not pity them. They are much closer to the kingdom than are the rich. Do not think that the end of life is worldly goods. It is the things of the world that blind us to the kingdom. But feed the hungry and care for the suffering as you would care for your own mother or father or wife or friend. Watch for the kingdom, for it is there, among the poor. The Glory is revealed among the homeless, for the Child of Adam has nowhere to lay his head."

> See Luke 6:20, 9:58

> Ye Su teaches responsibility for those in need, but not pity. We should not judge the worth or happiness of people by their worldly wealth. The kingdom is there among the poor. The rich may not, in fact, be "well-off" for they are likely be caught in the web of ego-craving and not even know it. On the other hand, the poor may just be free enough from the world to know the light.

35. Weep for the rich, for it is easier for a camel to pass through the eye of a needle than for a rich man to enter the kingdom.

> See Matthew 19:23-24.

---

[79] Rumi *op. cit.*, 175-176.

Compare: Scripture of the Western Ascension 6.23 "you must not pursue opulence...then you can attain eternal life."[80]

Like the biblical Jesus, Ye Su warns us about riches; yet how often have Christians really listened? It is interesting that throughout *The Secret Sayings* the author takes much more seriously the actual teachings of the canonical Jesus than do many other theologians.

Gandhi, who, I think, would strongly approve of *The Secret Sayings,* once wrote:

> A time is coming when those who are in the mad rush today of multiplying their wants, vainly thinking that they add to the real substance, the real knowledge of the world, will retrace their steps and say: "What have we done?' Civilizations have come and gone, and in spite of all our vaunted progress I am tempted to ask again and again, 'To what purpose?[81]

Throughout *The Secret Teachings* Ye Su speaks of the poor and the rich in worldly terms. He is certainly not happy with those who make worldly riches their goal. At the same time, his words must also be read "from the outside in." That is, what really matters is the poverty or richness of the inner life. He finds fulfillment, not in rich experience, but in the poverty of emptiness. The kingdom is not some thing to experience but No Thing at all.

Thus, salvation does not fill us but rather empties us. Ye Su does not come to offer ideas or feelings or sensations. The kingdom is not some special effect. Rather the ego must become like Rumi's sunrise ruby,[82] clarified so that it offers no resistance to the light. It is in the not knowing, in the emptiness, that illumination comes.

36. **The true gifts of the Magi I give you: compassion, simplicity, and dare not be first in the world.**

This surely is drawn from the *Dao De Jing* no. 67 that reads:

---

[80] Kohn, *op. cit.,* 239.

[81] As quoted in M.K. Gandhi, *Truth is God,* 127.

[82] Rumi, *The Essential Rumi,* 100.

I have three treasures.
Guard and keep them.
The first is compassion;
The second is frugality;
The third is daring not to be first in the world.[83]

I must confess that in my translation, I may have made the two passages read more alike than the Greek and Chinese actually do, but I am convinced that this text directly alludes to, if not quotes, the *Dao De Jing*. I believe a careful study of the Greek text will justify my translation.

37. **The kingdom is like an ancient well which flows with living water. Draw up the water and quench your thirst.**

See John 4:14

It seems likely that he drew this image as well as the use of the word *"Paygay"* from John's Gospel. If humans would know it, all their craving for power and riches is really only satisfied by this well of living water within.

38. **Trust in the kingdom. That is all that is needed.**

The word here translated "trust" is the imperative of pisteuo (πιστευω) that is often translated "believe" or "have faith in." Ye Su, however, radically de-emphasizes doctrines and word games. He in no way wishes to reduce faith to accepting certain ideas (See no. 49). Therefore, I think "trust" is a better translation. Finally, the kingdom for Ye Su is not a doctrine to believe in but a power to rely upon.

39. **From the Source flows the One and the One contains the Two. The Two give birth to the Third, the Child of Adam, and from the Three flow forth all things.**

Compare with the *Dao De Jing* no. 42

Tao produced One;
One produced Two;

---

[83] My translation.

Two produced Three;
Three produced the ten thousand things.[84]

The Source is that vast, divine Emptiness, beyond all comprehension. From it flows the One, the Primal Energy (qi: 氣). That energy then manifests itself as positive and negative energy (that is: yin and yang: 陰陽) that congeal into the universe (Heaven and Earth). The Child of Humanity (Adam) is born from Heaven and Earth and constitutes the third.

It was a commonplace in traditional China to regard the universe as made up of Heaven, Earth, and Humanity. Each creates. Humanity completes the universe by creating civilization.

40. **All flows creatively from the Source. When you create, the power of the Source is yours. Music, Poetry, Art are gifts from the Source.**

It is interesting that the author specifically sees the Arts as flowing forth from the Source. This doesn't mean that the Arts are pure or beyond ego-craving. The Arts, too, can be badly corrupted. Nevertheless, the spark of inspiration comes from, or perhaps is, the Source. Thus the Arts are of great value for returning to the Source, for they intimate the kingdom. William Blake would be very pleased with this saying, for he saw music, poetry, and art as the gift of Christ.[85]

41. **John said, "Teach us about the Spirit." Ye Su said, "The Spirit is the kingdom made manifest. When the trees move their branches you know that the Spirit is there. The Spirit is your life. When you breathe, it is the Spirit that moves within you. When your breath flows perfectly with the Spirit, you are in the kingdom. Watch your breath."**

See John 3:8

Like the kingdom, the Spirit is natural to us; it is our life. To return to pure breathing, to rid oneself of an unclean spirit, is to rediscover the kingdom. This passage would seem to point the follower toward the clas-

---

[84] My translation.
[85] See, for instance, S. Foster Damon, *Blake's Job*, 50-51.

sic meditation practices of both Daoism and Buddhism, for in each "watching the breath" is very important. It is noteworthy that here the usual Western dualism of spirit and flesh is discarded. The Spirit and the physical breath are directly intertwined if not one.

42. James said, "Our enemies surround us and want to destroy the kingdom. How shall we fight against our enemies? Shall we take up arms?" Ye Su said, "Love your enemies; do good to those who misuse you, for in them also dwells the kingdom. And forgive, always forgive." "But," said James, "suppose that they should try to kill us?" Ye Su replied, "No one can kill the kingdom for it has been from the beginning and will be until the end. As for the rest, it is mortal and will return to the Mother. Do not cling to life. Life and death are twin sisters who can never be separated. Death too is a blessing. But enter the kingdom where there is eternal life."

See Matthew 5:38-48

In the Sermon on the Mount, Jesus clearly emphasizes that his followers should eschew all fighting, all retaliation, for he says to "love your enemies," "turn the other cheek," "do good to those who despitefully use you." Christians generally have not only ignored these sayings but, at times, have attacked those believers, like the Quakers and various Anabaptists, who have tried to take them seriously. Although Christians have vowed obedience to Christ, they have often done so with fingers crossed, thinking his way impractical.

Leo Tolstoy, seeing the disparity between Jesus' teachings about non-violence and the actions of so-called Christian nations, wrote in his *The Law of Love and the Law of Violence:*

> "The peculiarity of the position of today's Christian nations is that they have founded their life on a teaching which in its true meaning destroys that life; and this hitherto concealed meaning is beginning to come to light. The Christian nations built their house not on sand but on ice. And the ice has begun to melt, has already melted, and the house will collapse."[86]

---

[86] Leo Tolstory, *A Confession and Other Religious Writings,* 167.

Ye Su, in this passage, emphasizes the teachings of non-violence found in the Sermon on the Mount. If you renounce all ego-craving, then protecting that ego is no longer important. You do not retaliate; you do not defend yourself, for death is inevitable anyway. Most people would reject such ideas as impractical, but one wonders whether wars, which have produced so much death and suffering are, after all, as practical as the pragmatists suggest.

Certainly Gandhi, Badshah Khan, and Martin Luther King, to mention a few modern examples, have shown us clearly that a philosophy of non-violence can be a powerful force for good in the world and is by no means based upon timidity or fear. Indeed, it is the ego-craving of the world that springs from deep-seated anxiety and fearfulness.

43. In all things be mindful.

This little statement certainly calls to mind much of the Buddha's teaching and is another hint about the author's meditational practice. In brief, it says, always be aware of what you are doing, thinking, saying. Don't let those ego-craving reflexes take over. Rely on the Source.

We have already encountered hints of what Yoga would call *pranayama* or breath control in no. 41, and *pratyahara* or withdrawal of the senses in no. 16. This passage could be construed as referring to *dharana* or concentration. The ending of no. 16 could also be interpreted as *samhadi* or ultimate trance. Thus, except for *asana* (posture) and perhaps *dhyana* (deep meditation), Ye Su teaches the basic steps in yogic practice.

44. "Is my soul immortal? Will I go to heaven?" asked John. "Your *psyche*," said Ye Su, "is a function of your body and like your body will return to dust. But the kingdom of light is everlasting. Enter the kingdom of light and find eternal *shalom*."

This, too, is very reminiscent of Buddhism. Ye Su does not teach the immortality of the soul, for the psyche (ψυχη), including your personality, is part of this ever-changing world and hence is not eternal. As the Buddha says, "All component parts decay." If something is made up of parts, it will eventually fall apart. What is eternal is the root of life, the Source. Ye Su teaches how to return to that Source through renunciation and the discipline of meditation to find eternal life.

Those who would regard such a position as heretical should remember that the Hebrew Scriptures offer no clear promise of life beyond death but, in fact, sometimes seem to teach the opposite. As God says in Genesis 3:19, "You are dust, and to dust you shall return." Much later in the Bible Qoheleth asked the pertinent question: "Who knows whether the spirit of man goes upward and the spirit of the beast goes down to the earth?" (Ecclesiastes 3:21)

I should also remark that I have rendered *eirene* (ειρηνη) as *shalom* rather than as "peace" because of the rich connotations of *shalom*. *Shalom*, a Hebrew word, implies not just the absence of conflict but wholeness, completeness, and a deep and abiding unity of Spirit.

45. I will die and on the third day will burst forth again from the tomb. The kingdom of light can be hidden for a time, but cannot be destroyed, not by the so-called religious authorities, not by the great world empires. If you trust in the kingdom, you will not fear death.

As in the canonical gospels, Ye Su predicts his own death and his victory over the grave. This author, however, does not indulge in stories of bodily rising or an empty tomb. What triumphs is the light, the kingdom that he has nourished and which Ye Su is.

46. Peter said, "Teacher, I hope and pray you will not die." Ye Su said, "If you wish to enter the kingdom, you must die, for new life comes only from death. Peter, all component parts decay. Your *psyche* will crumble into dust, but if your trust is into the light, you will rest in the light. Like me, you will burst forth again from the tomb. The light is eternal."

The word "into" translates the Greek *eis*. Like the New Testament, this text speaks of believing or trusting "into."

As usual Peter expresses the conventional belief, this time that death is a bad thing, Ye Su, however, takes a much more Buddhist point of view. In fact, the statement that "all component parts decay," is found in several sutras. In the *Mahaparinibbanasutta*, these are among the last words the Buddha speaks before he dies. Buddhists also strongly emphasize that the five *skandha* that make up the self fall apart at death. Thinking that somehow the personality is going to survive death is a good example of

ego-craving. When one has "seen through" the ego and its craving, however, one returns to the light and that light is eternal.

Although this view is similar in many ways to that of Laozi, it would
have been attacked by those Daoists who claimed, through various
elixirs, to be able to make the body immortal. More than one Chinese
Emperor died from doses of those elixirs in an attempt to live forever. Ye
Su would say that all such efforts to become immortal smack of ego-craving and should be avoided.

47. Judas said, "Teacher, the prophets taught us that the Eternal demands justice for all. Should we not organize to fight against the injustice in our society?" Ye Su said, "*Agape* demands justice in the world and woe to the person who does not seek to right the wrongs of society. But *agape* also knows
that justice without the kingdom is hollow and unstable. In this world of
craving, injustice will always reign because craving demands injustice. To
think that there can be true justice without the coming of the kingdom is
an illusion."

> Ye Su, in this passage, sets down the basis for a social ethic. Justice must
> be the aim of anyone who trusts in the Source, but we must also be aware
> that in this world of ego-craving justice is always infected by such crav-
> ing and therefore is always less than perfect. Injustice will always rule in
> social and economic realms until the kingdom has become a universal
> reality. Within this world, true justice can only be described, in the
> words of Reinhold Niebuhr, as an impossible possibility.[87]

48. The kingdom comes from the glory of the Eternal, Incomprehensible Source.

> In one sentence, the author sums up the whole teaching of the book.

49. Judas said, "Let us organize ourselves with a president and officers so that
our movement may be more effective." Ye Su said, "*Agape* does not hold to
order. The more you organize, the more your organization will become but
one more institution of craving. Soon you will have some men ruling over
others. Some will be forced to bow to their masters. There will be ordinances and taboos. People will begin to think that faith is just subscribing

---

[87] Reinhold Niebuhr, *An Interpretation of Christian Ethics*, 103-135.

to a set of ideas and the kingdom will become a fossil to be put upon the shelf along with all the other archaic doctrines. Then there will be persecutions and wars carried out in my name as the blind lead the blind into disaster. No, Judas, call no person Father or Rabbi or the Reverend or your Holiness. All of this comes from the craving of the world and will only end in violence and disorder. The kingdom comes as a miracle and miracles cannot be contained."

See Matthew 23:8

It may seem strange that Judas speaks of a president, a term which sounds very modern, but ancient synagogues had presidents[88] (see Matthew 9:18) and so I have translated the term that way. The Greek word has a variety of meanings, all of which denote, in some way, someone in authority. It may be significant that Judas, who otherwise is not regarded as an agent of evil in this work, is the one who asks about organization.

This seems to be a very strong reaction to a simple call for a little more organization, but, given the bloody history of Christianity, it is not ill-taken. Ye Su warns us that once one tries to organize the kingdom, the ego-cravings of the world begin to take over and, when that happens, violence and disorder are bound to be the result.

This is surely one of Ye Su's most telling objections to the "organized, visible Church." The question is whether this is a criticism of his own Church of the East or of the hierarchical Western Church that the author has experienced or heard about. Or, perhaps, it is a criticism of the organizations of Daoism and Buddhism that corrupted by their very existence the message of their "founders."[89] Whomever Ye Su has in mind, he is very sure that power and holiness do not mix. When the Holy Church gains power it cannot be any longer holy.

---

[88] Gerhard Kittel, *Theological Dictionary of the New Testament*, I. 488-489. The synagogue presidents were called in Greek *archisynagogos*.

[89] It is probably not legitimate to think of Laozi as the founder of Daoism.

50. When you meet, meet as friends. Love one another. Celebrate *agape*.

> The true Church is not an organization with powerful bishops *et al* but is simply friends, bound together by *agape*. Ultimately, the author is not at all against Christian fellowship. What he reacts to is the sort of hierarchical government that has characterized so much of Christendom. It is noteworthy that the Church of the East did not include in its canon the Pastoral Epistles upon which so much of the Western Church's structure is based. It was, nevertheless, quite hierarchical and consequently had many of the same problems that the Western churches had.

51. Proclaim the good news of the eternal kingdom but think not of proselytes. The kingdom will provide the miracle.

> Again, Ye Su speaks against the attitude of many Christians who wish to go out and convert the world to their ideas and their organization. There *is* good news, for return to the Source brings *agape*, joy and eternal life, but these are not found by either subscribing to a creed or joining an organization.

52. Do not think that a tribe or nation or empire can become the kingdom, for the kingdom will grow when and where it wills. Nothing will impede the kingdom more than a nation of addicts pretending to be the kingdom.

> For centuries after Constantine the Great made Christianity a *religio licita* of the Roman Empire, the Christian Church in the West sought to continue and expand that establishment. The Protestant Reformation, though it broke with Rome in some respects, continued and indeed elaborated the idea of the State Church and this led, of course, to persecutions and witch trials and religious wars. Ye Su will have none of this, warning strongly against the whole idea of Christendom as terribly corrupting. The Church, he implies, was far better off when it had no political power and was, in fact, persecuted.

53. I looked and I saw a great beast rising out of the earth, devouring everyone in its path. Great was its pride and great its claims to truth. To those whom it enticed it offered holy feelings and future hopes, but it attacked the very

kingdom it proclaimed. Those who were devoured seldom returned. The name of the beast was the Holy Church.

See Revelation 13.

In this most damning of sayings, Ye Su reveals to us that the so-called Holy Church actually attacks the very kingdom that Ye Su proclaims, for it replaces true renunciation with holy feelings and promises of heaven. Clearly the author is highly anti-ecclesiastical. Although particular events in his own experience may have led to this conclusion, this is actually a commentary on the relation between the spiritual and organized religion that could be applied to any tradition. If the coming of the kingdom is based upon a miracle, there is no way that the kingdom can be organized by humans.

54. **Keep my teachings secret; cast no pearls before swine, lest the great beast overhear the words and destroy.**

This saying, which incorporates Matthew 7:6, again explains the secrecy of these sayings. The beast, that is the Holy Church, would not like them at all, but then would adopt them only to corrupt them. One might suggest that this is exactly what happened to the teachings of Jesus.

55. **To live in the kingdom is to laugh and be glad. There is no soberness in the realm of light; it is freedom, hope, and joy.**

As usual, Ye Su is very positive about life. His Way has no grimness about it. It is the life of craving that brings grimness.

56. **I do not come to judge the world or anyone in it. I come to reveal the light of the kingdom. Those who turn from the light and seek the darkness condemn themselves and enter the darkness. Those who seek the light are of the light. Trust in the light and the healing is yours.**

See John 8:15

Ye Su arrives with no threats of judgment and hell. The life of craving is its own punishment. The world already experiences its own condemnation even though it may not recognize it as such. Ye Su comes to save, not to damn. His message is not so much an intellectual exercise as a healing "salve" to cure the human of that dread disease that we have called "ego-craving." Thus the salvation he offers is true spiritual health. Ye Su, like the Buddha, is a physician, not a propounder of theories.

57. **Do not judge others. If they seek the darkness, that is their danger, their woe. But trust the light and it will grow into a great flame. Let your light shine before all people that they may see and trust also.**

See: Matthew 7:1 and 5:16.
See also: The Third Liturgical Jesus Sutra: "So anyone who teaches the Triumphant Law practicing the Way of Light to bring life to the truth will know Peace and Happiness in company, but don't talk it away—this is the Way of No Virtue." [90]

Nos. 55, 56, and 57 provide a summary of his basic prescription for healing. The kingdom is characterized by freedom, hope, and joy. Walk in the light and judge no one. You proclaim the realm of light simply by depending on light and therefore living in freedom, hope, and joy, One is reminded of Jingjing's rules: no wanting, no doing, no piousness, no truth.

58. **James said, "There are other teachers in other lands who offer wisdom to the world. How should we think of them?" Ye Su said, "The seeds of the kingdom are everywhere. Do not think of the kingdom as your personal possession. My light is to be found everywhere in the world and many are those who have found me. But beware the influence of humanity's dark craving. Traditions of humanity are few that have not become corrupted by the craving. But where there is light, rejoice in it."**

This is a highly significant statement about understanding and relating to other religions. The light is not a possession of Christianity (as the Holy Church claims), nor is it even a possession of the man named Ye Su. The light, which comes from the Source, is everywhere. At the same time, every religion is infected by ego-craving and hence cannot be accepted simply at face value.

---

[90] Palmer, *op. cit.,* 199.

Compare this with the statement in what Palmer calls The Fourth Jesus Sutra: "All great teachers such as the Buddhas are moved by this Wind and there is nowhere in the world where this Wind does not reach and move."[91] The author of the *Secret Sayings,* however, also sees clearly just how corrupt all religions, including Buddhism and Daoism, could be.

59. One night Ye Su gathered those he taught and led them to an inner room set apart. There, at dinner, he took a loaf of bread and broke it before them, "This bread," he said "Is a gift from the Mother of us all. Together we share her matter. This loaf also comes from the sunlight of the Father's heavenly realm, now broken that we may become one in the heavenly light. Together we share the bread of heaven and earth; the kingdom of love is among us; this is my body."

60. The kingdom does not belong to individuals. It becomes manifest in *agape* shared. Therefore the loaf must be broken so that *agape* may be known in the sharing.

61. Ye Su also took a cup of wine, rich in aroma and body, and said, "This wine is a gift from our Mother to make glad the hearts of humans, so that we may know joy and *shalom.* It is likewise a gift from the sun from the Father's heavenly realm. It reminds us of the great transformation which the light and love of the kingdom bring. This is my blood poured out. In the world, wine may bring drunkenness; here one finds the kingdom."

See Matthew 26: 26-29, Mark 14: 22-26, Luke 22: 14-23.

It is interesting that the *Jesus Sutras* contain no mention of the Last Supper. Was this just an oversight or had the church given up Christianity's central sacrament? The *Secret Sayings* shows that the Eucharist may have been retained, but with a very different interpretation.

One should note the etymological connection between mater (mother) and matter. The Great Mother is matter, but, for the author, matter is not in any way connected with evil. Energy and Matter both arise out of the One that flows forth from the Source.

---

[91] Palmer, *op..cit.,* 160.

For an emphasis upon Heaven and Earth in the *Jesus Sutras* see: The Fourth Liturgical Sutra that begins:

> The highest skies are in love with You.
> The great Earth opens its palms in peace.[92]

This version of the Last Supper is significantly different from anything found in the canonical gospels. The bread and wine are the same, but now the author emphasizes that Heaven and Earth together (along with humans, of course) have produced the bread and the wine. The unity of Heaven and Earth is the unity of the Universe and the unity of the Universe is the Source. Thus, since Ye Su reveals the Source, they are analogous to and, in fact, are his body. Both also symbolize the Great Transformation which takes place through renunciation. Just as the bread rises and the wine ferments, so the light of heaven and the water from the well cause radical changes in the human spirit.

This passage also helps to explain why Ye Su so highly values marriage. Human marriage is the reenactment of the union of Heaven and Earth, of celestial energy and matter, of yin and yang. *Agape* is the source of this unity that, in turn, flows from the Source. It should also be noted that all this happens in an inner room, a clue that although this is the basis for an external rite it is also an "inner, spiritual event."

We cannot leave this passage without remembering once more Li Bo:

> Facing Wine
>
> Never refuse wine, I'm telling you,
> people come smiling in spring winds:
>
> peach and plum like old friends, their
> open blossoms scattering toward me,
>
> singing orioles in jade-green trees,
> and moonlight probing gold wine jars.

---

[92] *Ibid.*, 202.

Yesterday we were flush with youth,
and today, white hair's an onslaught,

Bramble's overgrown Shih-hu Temple,
and deer roam Ku-su Terrace ruins:

it's always been like this, yellow dust
choking even imperial gates closed

in the end. If you don't drink wine,
where are those ancient people now?[93]

62. **I am the True Light, glowing from the Eternal Source. Cleave the wood, I
am there; lift the stone, I am there.**

See John 1:9, 3:19 *et passim.*
See also: The Gospel of Thomas no. 77.

It seems quite significant that the author may have known the *Gospel
according to Thomas* as well as other apocryphal literature. This would
seem to indicate he may have been educated in West Asia, Egypt, or
Europe.

The author's Christology seems to be neither that of Nestorius nor of the
classical creeds. Here Ye Su *is* the kingdom that is the root of all of us, of
all existence. He is the Eternal Light, shining from all eternity; and therefore is entirely divine; yet he is entirely human, for to be truly human is
to be, at root, the Light. Ye Su comes to remind us of who we are, to
wake us up, to uncover the light that forever glows.

63. **Ye Su asked Mary, "What shall you do when I return from the dead?" Mary
said, "If you were to return from the dead, I would observe awe-struck
silence and speak to no one about it." Ye Su said, "You have learned well,
Mary. You shall be my apostle."**

This saying is reminiscent of what appears to have been the original ending of the Gospel of Mark :"And they went out and fled from the tomb;

[93] Li Po, *op. cit.,* 112.

for trembling and astonishment had come upon them; and they said nothing to any one, for they were afraid." Mark 16:8 Thus Mark ends, not with a great proclamation but with silence.

The author then, in no. 64, correlates this with a famous line from the *Dao De Jing*, no. 56. When Peter, in no. 65 protests that he needs to say *something*, Ye Su simply leads everyone in the Circular Dance of Joy, somewhat reminiscent of Jesus' remarks in *The Acts of John*, 94-96.[94] The message of the resurrection then is not a verbal one, for no one can comprehend that vision of light. One can only dance for joy; one can only be the light.

64. **Have you not heard that it was said of old, "Those who speak do not know, those who know do not speak."**

See: *Dao De Jing* no. 56.
Compare with The Third Liturgical Sutra's emphasis upon "no truth." "What does a mirror do? It reflects without judgment. And you—you should do likewise." [95]

Among the documents found in the Mogao caves is a work entitled *A Dialogue on the Contemplation-Extinguished*. Near the end of this Chan work, the pupil says to the teacher,

> "How good! My dear master, you have preached by not preaching. I have really heard by not hearing. Once hearing and preaching have come to be in accord with one another, all is calm and still without any words."[96]

The *Vimalakirtinirdesasutra* was one of the popular sutras during the Tang dynasty and was illustrated in the Mogao Caves. More than almost any other Mahayana sutra it emphasizes that the truth is beyond words. For instance, Vimalakirti says, "To teach the Dharma is presumptuous, and those who listen to it listen to presumption.[97]"

[94] Montague Rhodes James, *The Apocryphal New Testament*, 253-254.
[95] Palmer, *op. cit.,*199.
[96] Gishin Tokiwa, trans. *A Dialogue on the Contemplation-Extinguished*, 21.
[97] Vimilakirtinirdesasutra, *op. cit.* 25.

Clearly the author of *The Secret Sayings* is strongly influenced by this attitude. Ultimately, truth is beyond words. Talking about the kingdom is likely to corrupt it.

65. Peter said, "But we must say *something*. How can we proclaim the good news if we can say nothing?" Ye Su smiled but did not speak. Then he led his disciples in the Circular Dance of Joy that they danced until the dawn.

> See *The Acts of John*, 94-96. There are several Gnostic gospels in which Jesus dances.

> It is perhaps significant that so many churches were, for such a long time, opposed to dancing; yet it is in dance, the bodying forth of joy, that this author believes the gospel is best expressed. Faith is not just a mental thing; it involves the whole self, including the body. To trust the Source is to dance in thin air. To be against dance is to hate the body, the Mother, and thus the Source.

66. Ye Su hung upon the tree of life. He chanted the ancient psalms as blood dripped from his hands and feet. He spoke words of *shalom* to those who had not run away in fear. He encouraged and forgave. The earth trembled and the heavens grew dark. The Mother sobbed and the Father mourned. But in the midst of the trembling there was serenity; in the midst of darkness there was tremendous light streaming from every pore of his body, radiating to every corner of the earth. In death, life is born; in darkness, there is a dawning.

> Compare with the words of the great Stele: "The Religion of Light teachings are like the resplendent sun: they have the power to dissolve the dark realm and destroy evil forever." [98]
> The image of light streaming forth from every pore is very Buddhist. In Cave 61 of the Mogao Caves, for instance, there is a painting of a light-emitting Buddha. [99]

---

[98] Palmer, *op. cit.*, 226.
[99] *The Art Treasures of Dunhuang*, mural no. 110, and p. 236.

This passage expresses the paradox to which the whole collection of say-ings points. Horror and peace, light and darkness, life and death are one. In a sense, the death and resurrection of Ye Su are not two events but an indivisible unity. This is the paradox of paradoxes, the clue to all. The life of the kingdom is not found by moving from death to life but in finding life in death and death in life. An event that is violent and ugly beyond belief is, in the very same instant, a revelation of everything that is pure and holy. Craving and enlightenment are one.

67. **Death came, the tomb was made ready and then, after the burial, sealed. But nothing can hold the light. At any moment it can burst forth with an unimaginable radiance. And it does.**

No angels, no stone rolled away: just unimaginable radiance bursting forth. The story must be read, not as an historical narrative, but as an inner transformation that brings the Peace and Happiness that the Third Liturgical Sutra so emphasizes. For the author of *The Secret Sayings*, the whole of the gospel must be understood "from the outside in." That is to say, the gospel story should be taken, not as history but as a parable of the inner life. To take it as history is to miss the whole point. To avoid that common Christian misunderstanding, the author simply omits the history to let us see what the gospel is really about.

68. **And you must die. Your craving, born of your prideful ego, must perish. Your death, like that of Ye Su, will be dreadfully painful, for the addiction is so intense and has gone on so long. Earth will tremble and Heaven will grow dark before the veil is rent, the Holy of Holies revealed, and the light, the eternal light, begins to shine.**

See Mark 8:34-35.

The *Secret Sayings* record the death and resurrection of Jesus, but the whole historical framework is missing. Pontius Pilate, the Jews, Jerusalem are no longer needed as the author emphasizes the central, spiritual core of the story. There is no empty tomb, no physical body, no ascension up into the skies. The resurrection is an outpouring of the light that is eternal. It is a story of the death of the self in renunciation and its rebirth in the Spirit.

As in the *Jesus Sutras* there is no mention here of divine forgiveness as the central meaning of the crucifixion and resurrection. The theme is rather one of transformation. It should noted, however, that the canonical gospels do not emphasize free divine forgiveness either. In fact, Jesus tells us that we should only expect to be forgiven in so far as we forgive others. Therefore, rather than beginning worship with a confession of sin and absolution, Christians ought to begin by offering forgiveness to others from the heart.

In previous passages, *The Secret Sayings* seems to speak to no one in particular. Now, in no. 68, the author turns and directly addresses the reader. This message is not meant for someone else. It is meant for you!

69. The Well, the Water, and the Drink of Eternity: the three are one.

Clearly, this is an attempt to restate the doctrine of the Trinity in a bold new way. In so doing, the author returns to the metaphor of the spring (πηγη) that dominated so much of the first half of this work. Here the doctrine of the Trinity is stripped of all its pseudo-philosophical vocabulary. To know the so-called Trinity is simply to drink from the spring of living water.

70. I Am the Way, the Truth, and the Life. In every part of the world those who know, know me. I am the wise man's treasure and the lost man's refuge.

See John 14:06
Compare *Dao De Jing*, no. 62.

The author knows what many readers of John have forgotten: that the Word (λογος) is a cosmic reality that has been from the beginning and exists everywhere. When Jesus says, "I am the Way, the Truth and the Life," he speaks as the universal Word, as the Word that every person who has renounced hears, the treasure that those who seek find.
Again, the words of Han Shan:

> In the old days when I was so poor,
> Night after night I counted other men's wealth.
> Recently I thought it over
> And decided to open a business of my own.
> I dug a hole and found a hidden treasure—

A store of crystal jewels.
A blue-eyed foreigner came in secret
And wanted to buy them and take them away,
But I only answered him,
"These jewels are beyond price!"[100]

The treasure that Han Shan found buried, of course, is the treasure of great price, the kingdom that Ye Su proclaims.

71. **To you I leave the gifts of the Spirit: *agape,* simplicity, and *shalom.* The kingdom of light is here. It is time to rejoice.**

When the powers of craving have been overcome, a new world opens. It has always been there, but craving hides it. It is the life in which love, simplicity, and peace prevail; it is the life of the true human. There could be nothing more wonderful than this. In the words of the apostle Paul, "Rejoice in the Lord always; again I will say, rejoice." (Philippians 4:4)

It is not, however, that there is some thing to hope for or rejoice in. The kingdom is not a matter of waiting for some cosmic Christmas to come. The kingdom itself is hope and joy. It is now.

The Dhammapada, an ancient Buddhist text, expresses much the same experience:

O let us live in joy, in love amongst those who hate! Among men who hate, let us live in love.
O let us live in joy, in health amongst those who are ill! Among men who are ill, let us live in health.
O let us live in joy, in peace amongst those who struggle! Among men who struggle, let us live in peace.
O let us live in joy, although having nothing! In joy let us live like spirits of light.[101]

---

[100] Han Shan, *Cold Mountain,* 77.
[101] *The Dhammapada,* 64.

72. **Take care to whom these words are given, for those of the world will laugh and deride and then use them for their own worldly ends. Hide my secrets until the time is fulfilled. Beware the beast.**

> See Mark 1:15 which uses the same phrase "the time is fulfilled. "Mark's meaning, however, is no clearer than it is here. An alternative translation might be, "the season is over."

> The author closes as he began, with a warning. If the ego-craving world receives this book, it will be turned into another ego-craving religion. That is what happened to Daoism, to Buddhism, and to Christianity. Therefore, he tells us to hide the secrets until the time is fulfilled. Is this an apocalyptic statement, anticipating the end of time as we know it, or is it meant to be taken on a much more personal level? That is to say, the author could mean that the text must wait for some eschatological change in society, or he might mean that the text should not be revealed until an individual is ready to receive it. The author is really not clear on this point. Perhaps the lack of clarity is intentional. What is clear is that the author is aware of how easily the message of this work can be corrupted. Like Jesus, he knows what happens when you offer pearls to pigs.

Concluding Matters

Why was this Text Written in Greek?

Finally, we must address a most difficult question: Why was this work, so obviously a synthesis of Christian and Chinese thought, written in Greek? This is a problem that has perplexed me ever since I first began my work of translation. I have entertained several hypotheses:

1. Perhaps this work was written by a missionary from the West who was consciously attempting to restate the gospel in Chinese terms, as a way of converting the Chinese to Christianity. It is possible his attitude toward an established church indicates that he was familiar with the Western Church and its problems. The difficulty with this theory is that, in the first place, the missionaries from the Church of the East would have used Syriac, not Greek.[102] At a somewhat earlier date one could imagine this to have been someone from the Greek colony of Bactria, but by the seventh century, there were few Greek speakers left there. It is true, of course, that the author could have been someone from Byzantium, but then the question is: why is the Greek so much like that of the New Testament? I doubt that I could have translated seventh century Byzantine Greek at all. Would someone from seventh or eighth century Byzantium have written in Greek like this?

2. This was written by a Christian in China who was going to send it (or perhaps did send a copy of it) back to one of the Churches of the West. If that is so, however, why would he use the name Ye Su without inflection rather than the usual "Jesus?" Surely, also, the author would have known that many of the ideas expressed here would have been regarded as sheer heresy both in the West and in the Church of the East. Just as the Catholic priest who first was asked to translate the work found it quite heretical, so too would most representatives from either the Roman Catholic or Orthodox communions. New documents that put words in the mouth of Jesus would have been regarded as heretical. Nor would this document, because of its positive attitudes toward matter and the body, have found much favor among whatever Gnostic groups still existed.

---

[102] It is true that at an earlier time students at Nisibis, the famous Church of the East theological school, would have studied Greek, but by the first decade of the seventh century that school had come to an end. Gillman and Klimkeit, 114, 124.

I was, quite frankly, perplexed. Nothing seemed to make good sense. And then I read once more the final line of the text. "**Hide my secrets until the time is fulfilled. Beware the beast.**" Could it be that the text was written in Greek precisely to hide its secrets? Perhaps the author had studied Greek in order to read the New Testament in the original. Therefore, he wrote textbook, *koine* Greek, the kind I can read. And he did so because he did not want his fellow Christians, who could not read Greek, to read the text, at least not until the time was right. Perhaps when he was active, he translated the text orally for initiates who were ready. Then, before his death, he hid the text more permanently, with the belief that some day it would be discovered and deciphered by people who would understand.

And the scroll remained hidden for some thirteen hundred years, waiting for the right time, for an age that might regard with more favor this startling fusion of East and West, this deeply spiritual and anti-hierarchical message. As I think about that strange and wonderful thought, the question emerges: is this the right time? Should I even publish this? Are we ready for the new wine that this gospel offers? Is this really Jesus speaking to us today? Read the text again for yourself. See what you think.

Further Conclusions

Now that we have examined the text and placed it in at least a plausible context, it is time to come to some conclusions about the author, his or her background, and approximately when this text could have been written.

Let us begin by considering the time of the author. As we have shown, the author of the *Secret Sayings* was profoundly influenced by both Buddhism and Daoism and shows many affinities with the *Jesus Sutras*. With each of these documents, the *Secret Sayings* shows some close relationships, though in the end it is unique and quite different from all others. Nevertheless, it seems to me that the similarities are enough to place the *Secret Sayings* within the context of Tang Dynasty China.

At the same time, *The Secret Sayings* represents a stage in development that is quite sophisticated, certainly much more sophisticated than the first Jesus Sutra with which the *Sayings* bears marked resemblance. The author's rather strident comments about religious organizations also seem to imply bitter experience with such organizations but whether within or without the Chinese milieu is not certain. Finally, the work's apparent sympathies with Chan Buddhism also probably mean a date somewhat removed from the 635 C.E. entry date. It is for these reasons that I would suggest an eighth century date, perhaps even later than Jingjing, though one could imagine them as contemporaries.

Who was this author? Although the author is surely well acquainted with Chinese thought and is speaking to a Chinese audience, there are also strong indications that he may have come to China from the West. First of all, he knows not only the canonical gospels but refers to the Gospel of Thomas and probably the Acts of John. Did people in China or even Persia know these non-canonical works? Secondly, the author knows Greek, at least of a basic sort. How many people in China or even in Persia at that time could read and write in *koine* Greek?

Therefore, I would suggest that if this person did not come from West Asia, Egypt, or Europe, he or she[103] may very well have studied there. Because of the author's antipathy toward the Holy Church, it could well be that the author had had trouble with the established Western Church and had fled east to China. There, trouble with other religious traditions only confirmed the idea that religious organization is itself an evil to avoid.

All of this is, of course, quite speculative. Once the original scroll is examined very different conclusions may result. My own deductions, however, seem, at this stage, plausible. The author is a refugee from a world where religion is tied to political rule, a world that corrupts the gospel for its own ends. After a long journey he arrives in China and discovers a whole new spiritual outlook on life as well as the same old problems of organized religion. This work contains the author's mature and deep reflections upon the meaning of the gospel in this new world. But even in China, because his thoughts were radical, he felt it necessary to keep them secret from all but his closest and most trusted friends. Perhaps, like a good Chan Buddhist or Daoist he, by writing in Greek, spoke without speaking. Today, however, his thoughts are revealed anew and he proves himself to be one of the great spiritual teachers, not only of the Religion of Light, but of all time.

---

[103] Although a woman certainly could have written this, I will sometimes, for brevity's sake, refer to the author as "he."

Epilogue

Epilogue

Even though the stipulated time has elapsed and I am now free to publish *The Secret Sayings*, I have hesitated. Is it worthwhile to publish a translation when the original is so mysteriously unavailable. Certainly, the publication of the original Greek text is needed before scholars can accurately date and place this document historically. Undoubtedly, once the Greek text is uncovered, scholars may also dispute some of my translations. Therefore, I again want to urge Messrs Wang and Chang, wherever they are, to come forward with the original text so that scholarly work may proceed. It is my profound hope that they are alive and well and they were not imprisoned or otherwise punished for their attempt to make this document available to the world.

As I have already said, however, there is a positive side to the absence of the original. There is a danger that this document, like so many others, will eventually be scrutinized and catalogued historically, interpreted and understood according to whatever context it may have come from, and then left for the erudite to dispute about.

Without such historical analysis, we are freer to interpret and understand *The Secret Sayings of Ye Su* for itself, as a work that transcends time, with a message for all who have ears to hear. Perhaps the lack of the original document saves it from the scholarly ego-craving which has muted so many other works from the past and which the author most certainly would have deplored.

I myself find it eerie that such a document may have been written, as it were, "in code" and hidden away until the time was right for discovery. The question I have asked in this work several times is whether the time is right at all. Are there any ears today to hear this document? Should I not let the text sleep longer in secret?

Today, all forms of Christianity, perhaps of all religions, seem to be reaching the end of a long era. Many factors, both intellectual and social, have eaten away the fabric of religious traditions. Many have said that churches must either change or die. Does this text, so long hidden in the darkness of some Chinese cave, help? Can it point the way to a new and very different sort of spirituality?

It seems to me that this work is not just one for the scholars but for the spiritually awake. I could imagine *The Secret Sayings* becoming the basis for a whole new form of spiritual engagement, a way that transcends sects and schisms and indeed transcends religion itself. The author, however, would be the last person to want to form yet one more religious organization. That indeed has always been the problem. The light emerges; societies are formed; then the squabbling begins.

The world, to be frank, has no need of any more societies that claim the truth and look for members. What the world needs is a drink from that fountain of Living Water. What it needs is a glimpse of that Eternal Light shining in the darkness, radiating to every corner of the earth. What we all yearn to do is to return to the Source from which existence flows. How can this happen without spinning off yet one more church to compete for membership? I will be interested to learn what others think.

I cannot close this book without one more word from the poet Kabir:

> The whole world
> is enthralled by Maya;
> this same Maya
> has drowned whole families.
>
> O man, how did you wreck
> your raft in such a wide, clear place?
> Because you broke away from Hari,
> and hooked on Maya.
>
> Gods and men burn;
> the fire blazes.
> Water is so near,
> yet the beasts don't drink.
>
> By meditating, by meditating,
> the water sprang forth,
> "That water is pure,"
> says Kabir.[104]

---

[104] Kabir, *op. cit.*, 55.

Works Cited

Works Cited

Allen, Sarah. *The Way of Water and Sprouts of Virtue* (Albany: State University of New York Press, 1997).

Art Treasures of Dunhuang/compiled by the Dunhuang Institute for Cultural Relics, The (New York: Lee Publishers Group, Inc., 1981).

Bhagavad-gita, The. Translated by Barbara Stoller Miller (New York: Bantam Books, 1986).

Bokenkamp, Stephen R. *Early Daoist Scriptures* (Berkeley: University of California Press, 1997).

Broughton, Jeffrey L. *The Bodhidharma Anthology* (Berkeley: University of California Press, 1999).

Buddhist Suttas . Translated by T. W. Rhys Davids (New York: Dover Publications, 1969).

Chang Po-Tuan, *Understanding Reality: A Taoist Alchemical Classic by Chang Po-Tuan with a Concise Commentary by Liu I-Ming*. translated by Thomas Cleary(Honolulu: University of Hawaii Press, 1987).

Cold Mountain: 100 poems by the T'ang poet Han-shan. Translated by Burton Watson (New York: Columbia University Press, 1970).

Cook, Francis H. *Hua-Yen Buddhism: The Jewel Net of Indra* (University Park: Pennsylvania State University Press, 1981).

Damon, S. Foster. *Blake's Job* (Hanover: University Press of New England, 1966).

Dhammapada, The Path of Perfection. Translated by Juan Mascaro (New York: Penguin Books, 1973).

Dialogue on the Contemplation-Extinguished, A. Translated by Gishin Tokiwa (The Institute for Zen Studies, 1973).

Dumolin, Heinrich. *Zen Buddhism: A History: Volume I, China and India* (New York: Macmillan, 1988).

Eberhard, Wolfram, *A History of China* (Berkeley: University of California Press, 1977).

Ebrey, Patricia Buckley and Peter N. Gregory, eds. *Religion and Society in T'ang and Sung China* (Honolulu: University of Hawaii Press, 1993),

Ennin, *Diary; The Record of a Pilgrimage to China in Search of the Law,*. Translated by Edwin O. Reischauer (New York: Ronald Press Co., 1955).

Foltz, Richard C. *Religions of the Silk Route: Overland Trade and Cultural Exchange from Antiquity to the Fifteenth century* (New York: St. Martin's Press, 1999).

Foster, John. *The Nestorian Tablet and Hymn: Translations of Chinese texts from the First period of the Church in China, 635-c900 (London: Society for Promoting Christian Knowledge, 1939).*

Gandhi, M. K. *The Bhagavadgita* (New Delhi: Orient Paperbacks, 1989).

Gandhi, M. K. *Truth is God.* Compiled by R.K. Prabhu (Ahmedabad: Navajivan Publishing House, 1955).

Gernet, Jacques. *A History of Chinese Civilization*, 2nd ed. (New York: Cambridge University Press, 1996).

Gillman, Ian and Hans-Joachim Klimkeit, *Christians in Asia Before 1500* (Ann Arbor: University of Michigan Press, 1999).

Grant, Asahel. *The Nestorians; or the Lost Tribe: containing evidence of their identity; an account of their manners, customs, and ceremonies; together with sketches of travels in ancient Assyria, Armenia, Media, and Mesopotamia; and illustrations* (New York: Harper Brothers, 1841).

Hatch, William Henry Paine. *The Principal Uncial Manuscripts of the New Testament* (Chicago: University of Chicago Press, 1939).

Holy Bible, The. Revised Standard Version (New York: Oxford University Press, 1962).

Holy Teaching of Vimalakirti The. Translated by Robert A. F. Thurman (University Park: Pennsylvania State University Press, 1986).

Hui Neng, *The Platform Sutra of the Sixth Patriarch,* Translated and introduced by Philip B. Yampolsky (New York: Columbia University Press, 1967).

James, Montague Rhodes, *The Apocryphal New Testament* (New York: Oxford University Press, 1924).

Kabir, *Songs of Kabir from the Adi Granth.* Translated by Nirmal Dass (New York: State University of New York Press, 1991).

Kierkegaard, Soren. *Fear and Trembling and The Sickness Unto Death.* Translated by.Walter Lowrie (New York: Doubleday Anchor Books, 1954).

Kittel, Gerhard. *Theological Dictionary of the New Testament* (Grand Rapids: Wm. B. Eerdmans Publishing Co., 1964).

Kohn, Livia. *Taoist Mystical Philosophy, The Scripture of the Western Ascension* (New York: State of New York University Press, 1991).

Ko Hung. *Alchemy, Medicine, and Religion in China of A.D. 320: The Nei P'ien of Ko Hung* Translated by James R, Ware (New York: Dover Publications, 1966).

Laozi. *The Guiding Light of Lao Tzu.* Translated and edited by Henry Wei (Wheaton, Ill.: The Theosophical Publishing House, 1982).

Lin Chi, *The Zen Teachings of Master Lin-Chi.* Translated by Burton Watson (Boston: Shambala, 1993).

Li Po, *The Selected Poems of Li Po.* Translated by David Hinton (New York: New Directions, 1996).

Lotus Sutra, The,. Translated by Burton Watson (New York: Columbia University Press, 1993).

.Moffett, Samuel Hugh. *A History of Christianity in Asia*, Vol. I: Beginnings to 1500 (Maryknoll, N.Y.: Orbis Books, 1998).

Niebuhr, Reinhold. *An Interpretation of Christian Ethics* (New York: Harper and Brothers Publishers, 1934).

Palmer, Martin. *The Jesus Sutras: Recovering the Lost Scrolls of Taoist Christianity* (New York: Ballantine Wellspring, 2001).

Po Chu-I, Selected Poems. Translated by Burton Watson (New York: Columbia University Press, 2000).

Red Pine. *The Zen Teaching of Bodhidharma* (San Francisco: North Point Press, 1987).

Robinet, Isabelle. *Taoism: Growth of a Religion* (Stanford, California: Stanford University Press, 1992).

Rumi, Jelaluddin, *The Essential Rumi*, Translated by Coleman Barks (San Francisco: Harper San Francisco, 1995).

Ryokan: Zen Monk-Poet of Japan. Translated by Burton Watson (New York: Columbia University Press, 1977),

Saeki, P.Y. *The Nestorian Monument in China* (London: SPCK, 1916).

Schafer, E.H. The Jade Woman of Great Mystery," *History of Religions* 17 (1978): 387-98.

Schipper, Kristofer. "Taoism: the Story of the Way." in Stephen Little with Shawn Eichman, *Taoism and the Arts of China* (Chicago: The Art Institute of Chicago, 2000), 42.

Suzuki, D.T. *Studies in the Lankavatara Sutra* (London: George Routledge and Sons, 1930).

T'ien-T'ai Buddhism: An Outline of the Fourfold Teachings, edited by David W. Chappell (Tokyo: Daiichi-Shobo, 1983).

Tolstory, Leo. *A Confession and Other Religious Writings* (New York: Penguin Books, 1987).

Twichett, Denis, ed.. *Sui and T'ang China, 589-906.*Part *I*, Vol. 3 of *The Cambridge History of China* (Cambridge: Cambridge University Press, 1979).

Twitchett, Denis and Michael Loewe, *The Ch'in and Han Empires* Vol. I of *The Cambridge History of China* (Cambridge: Cambridge University Press, 1986.

Weinstein, Stanley. *Buddhism Under the T'ang* (New York: Cambridge University Press, 1987).

Whitfield, Roderick and Anne Farrer. *Caves of the Thousand Buddhas: Chinese Art from the Silk Route* (New York: George Braziller Inc.,1990).

Wile, Douglas. *Art of the Bedchamber: The Chinese Sexual Yoga Classics including Women's Solo Meditation Texts* (Albany: State University of New York, 1992).

Wilson, Thomas. "Sacrifice and the Imperial Cult of Confucius," *History of Religions* 41.3 (Feb. 2002).

Wright, Arthur F. "T'ang T'ai-tsung and Buddhism," in *Perspectives on the T'ang* Edited by Arthur F. Wright and Denis Twichett (New Haven: Yale University Press, 1973), 239-265.

Wu, John C. H. *The Golden Age of Zen* (New York: Doubleday, 1996).

About the Author

Dr. Jay G. Williams. Walcott-Bartlett Professor of Religious Studies at Hamilton College holds advanced degrees from Union Theological Seminary in New York (M.Div) and Columbia University (Ph.D). He is the author of nine books, including *Yeshua Buddha, The Riddle of the Sphinx,* and *The Times and Life of Edward Robinson* as well as many journal articles, book reviews and chap books. His teaching emphasizes south and east Asian philosophy and religion.

0-595-33684-1

Printed in the United States
29715LVS00005B/388

9 780595 336845